S0-AVD-415

Apollo for
Adobe® Flex™ Developers
Pocket Guide

Mike Chambers, Robert L. Dixon,
and Jeff Swartz

O'REILLY®

Beijing · Cambridge · Farnham · Köln · Paris · Sebastopol · Taipei · Tokyo

Adobe Apollo® for Flex™: Pocket Guide
by Mike Chambers, Robert L. Dixon, and Jeff Swartz

Copyright © 2007 Adobe Systems, Inc. All rights reserved.
Printed in the United States of America.

Published by O'Reilly Media, Inc., 1005 Gravenstein Highway North, Sebastopol, CA 95472.

O'Reilly books may be purchased for educational, business, or sales promotional use. Online editions are also available for most titles (*safari.oreilly.com*). For more information, contact our corporate/institutional sales department: (800) 998-9938 or *corporate@oreilly.com*.

Editor: Steve Weiss	**Cover Designer:** Karen Montgomery
Production Editor: Philip Dangler	**Interior Designer:** David Futato
Indexer: Joe Wizda	**Illustrators:** Robert Romano and Jessamyn Read

Printing History:

March 2007:   First Edition.

ISBN-10: 0-596-51391-7
ISBN-13: 978-0-596-51391-7
[C]

Contents

Preface

This book provides a quick introduction to developing applications for the public Alpha 1 build of Adobe Apollo, a new cross-platform desktop application runtime. While Apollo allows both Flash- and HTML-based application development, this book focuses on building Apollo applications using the Adobe Flex Framework.

The book gives an overview of Apollo, shows how to set up your development environment, and discusses new Apollo functionality and APIs. Once you finish reading, you should have a good understanding of what Apollo is and how to build Flex-based applications for it.

Apollo Runtime Naming Conventions

The Apollo runtime allows developers to leverage a number of web technologies to deploy web applications to the desktop. Indeed, there are so many technologies, that it can be difficult to keep track of them all. The table below lists the terms used in the book, and what is meant by each one:

Name	Meaning
Apollo	The cross-platform desktop runtime that enables the running of Apollo Applications.
Apollo Application	An application built with Flash, HTML and/or PDF that runs on top of Apollo.

Name	Meaning
Flash	Any content contained within a SWF 9 file format that runs in the Flash Player or Apollo.
ActionScript	The ECMAScript-based programming language used to program Flash content. Unless otherwise noted, all mentions in this book refer to ActionScript 3.
HTML	Standard web-based markup language used to create and layout web pages.
JavaScript	Web-based implementation of ECMA Script used to program content within HTML applications.
PDF	Portable Document Format that allows for seamless distribution and display of electronic documents.
Flex Framework	An XML- and ActionScript-based Framework designed to make developing Flash-based Rich Internet applications easy. All discussions of the Flex Framework in the book refer to Flex 2.0 or greater.
Flex Builder	An Eclipse-based IDE used to build Flash-based Rich Internet Applications using Flex and ActionScript.

What This Book Covers

This book gives a general overview of what Apollo is, shows how to set up your development environment to start building applications, focuses on a couple of the new Apollo APIs (HTML and File), and finally, shows how to do a number of common programming tasks within Apollo.

As a general rule, features and functionality already in the alpha build are relatively stable and should not change radically (although they may be tweaked based on developer feedback). Any details discussed around unimplemented features and functionality are much more tentative and more likely to change in future builds.

It is also important to note that the Alpha 1 build of Apollo is not feature complete, and a number of significant Apollo features have not been implemented and/or included in the build.

The list below contains a partial list of features and functionality included in the Apollo Alpha 1:

- Mac support (OS X 10.4 (Intel and PPC)
- Windows support (Windows XP and Windows Vista Home Premium Edition)
- Application installation
- File I/O API
- All functionality within Flash Player 9, including complete network stack
- Windowing APIs (not complete)
- Command-line tools (ADL and ADT)
- HTML within Flash content
- Top-level HTML applications
- ActionScript/JavaScript Script bridging
- Flex Builder and Flex Framework support for authoring Apollo application
- Application command-line arguments
- Application icons

The list below contains a partial list of features planned for Apollo 1.0. These were not included in Alpha 1.

- PDF support
- Cross-platform menu API
- Right-click and contextual menu control
- Full HTML support
- System notifications
- Offline data API
- Drag-and-drop
- Rich clipboard access
- File type association

We will highlight any features that we know may change in future builds.

What Alpha Means

As the previous section shows, the Apollo Alpha 1 build is far from feature complete, and some the the features are only partially implemented. Thus, the implementation of specific features or availablity of any particular feature is subject to change dramatically between the Alpha build and 1.0 release.

This also applies to the information within this book. The book was written before the Alpha 1 build was finalized and thus it is possible that some of the APIs or features may have changed between those times. This is particularly the case with API names. If something isn't working as the book suggests it should, make sure to check the online documentation, which will always have the latest information on the Alpha 1 APIs.

You can find the latest information and documentation on Apollo at:

http://www.adobe.com/go/apollo

Audience for This Book

We hope that this book is for you, but just to be sure, let's discuss some of the assumptions that we made, as well as what type of developers the book is targeted at.

What Does This Book Assume?

The book assumes that the reader has at least a basic familiarity with creating Flash-based applications and content using the Flex Framework and ActionScript 3.0.

You should be familiar with web technologies such as Flash, Flex, HTML and JavaScript, as well as general web development concepts.

Who This Book Is For

This book is for developers interested in leveraging the Flex Framework to build and deploy Flash-based applications to the desktop via Apollo. If you don't have any experience with developing with the Flex Framework, then we suggest that you at least view some of the Flex introductory information and videos available at:

http://www.adobe.com/go/flex

Who This Book Is Not For

While it is possible to create HTML- and JavaScript-based applications with Alpha 1 of Apollo, this book does not go into any detail on HTML- and JavaScript-focused Apollo application development. If you are an HTML and JavaScript developer interested in building Apollo applications, then this book can provide a good introduction and overview of Apollo and its functionality, but you should view the Apollo documentation and articles available from the Apollo web site for a more HTML/JavaScript-focused discussion.

How This Book Is Organized

This book contains the following chapters and appendixes:

Chapter 1, *Introduction to Apollo*
    General overview of what Apollo is, and the types of applications it targets.

Chapter 2, *Getting Started with Apollo Development*
    Tips on starting your Apollo development, and the steps toward creating your first Apollo application.

Chapter 3, *Using HTML Within Flex-Based Apollo Applications*
    Discusses how HTML can be leveraged within Flash-based applications, and covers JavaScript/ActionScript communication via script bridging.

Chapter 4, *Using the File System API*
> Provides an introduction to the File API within Apollo, and how to use both synchronous and asynchronous APIs.

Chapter 5, *Apollo Mini-Cookbook*
> Provides tips and tricks for accomplishing common tasks within Apollo applications, presented in the O'Reilly Cookbook format.

Appendix A, *Apollo Packages and Classes*
> Provides a list of new or modified Apollo APIs added to ActionScript.

Appendix B, *Apollo Command-Line Tools*
> Provides a list of Apollo-specific command-line tools and their usage options.

How to Use This Book

This book can be used both as an introduction to and overview of Apollo, as well as a step-by-step guide to getting started with Apollo application development. While it may be tempting to jump ahead to specific sections, it is strongly suggested that you are least read the first two chapters, which provide an overview of Apollo, and discuss how to set up your development environment for building Apollo applications. This will make it much easier to then jump into the specific areas of Apollo functionality in which you are interested.

Once you have read through the book and understand the basics of how to build a Flex-based Apollo application, then you can use it as a reference, referring to specific sections when you need to know how to tackle a specific problem. In particular, the File, HTML, and Cookbook sections should prove useful as you develop Apollo applications.

Finally, this book is just an introduction to Apollo and does not cover all of the features and functionality included within it. It is meant to complement, but not replace, the extensive and in-depth documentation on Apollo provided by Adobe. Try to at least glance over the Apollo documentation to make sure that you are familiar with all of the APIs and functionality not covered in this book.

Conventions Used in This Book

The following typographical conventions are used in this book:

Plain text
> Indicates menu titles, menu options, menu buttons, and keyboard accelerators (such as Alt and Ctrl).

Italic
> Indicates new terms, URLs, email addresses, filenames, file extensions, pathnames, directories, and Unix utilities.

Constant width
> Indicates commands, options, switches, variables, attributes, keys, functions, types, classes, namespaces, methods, modules, properties, parameters, values, objects, events, event handlers, XML tags, HTML tags, macros, the contents of files, or the output from commands.

Constant width bold
> Shows commands or other text that should be typed literally by the user.

Constant width italic
> Shows text that should be replaced with user-supplied values.

License and Code Examples

This work, including all text and code samples, is licensed under the Creative Commons Attribution-Noncommercial-Share Alike 2.5 License.

To view a copy of this license, visit *http://creativecommons. org/licenses/by-nc-sa/2.5/*; or, (b) send a letter to Creative Commons, 543 Howard Street, 5th Floor, San Francisco, California, 94105, USA.

You can find more information on Creative Commons at *http://www.creativecommons.org*.

Support and More Information

Accessing the Book Online

You can always find the latest information about this book, as well as download free electronic versions of it from the book's web site at:

http://www.adobe.com/go/apolloflexpocketguide

Online Apollo Resources

Although Apollo is a new technology, there are already a number of resources where you can find more information on Apollo and Rich Internet Application development.

Apollo site

Primary web site for information, downloads, and documentation of Apollo:

http://www.adobe.com/go/apollo

Apollo Developer FAQ

Official Apollo FAQ answering common questions about Apollo:

http://www.adobe.com/go/apollofaq

Apollo Developer Center

Developer Center with articles, information, and resources on developing Applications for Apollo:

http://www.adobe.com/go/apollodevcenter

Apollo API Reference

Apollo ActionScript 3 API Reference:

http://www.adobe.com/go/apolloapi

Apollo Documentation

Complete Apollo Documentation:

http://www.adobe.com/go/apollodocs

Apollo Forum

Official Adobe Forum for discussing Apollo:

http://www.adobe.com/go/apolloforums

Apollo coders mailing list

Mailing list for discussing Apollo application development:

http://www.adobe.com/go/apollolist

Mike Chambers weblog

Mike Chambers' weblog. This author and member of the Apollo team posts frequently on Apollo:

http://www.adobe.com/go/mikechambers

MXNA Apollo Smart Category

Apollo Smart Category that lists any discussions about Apollo within the Adobe online development community:

http://www.adobe.com/go/apollomxna

Flex Developer Center

Developer Center with articles, information, and resources on working with the Flex Framework:

http://www.adobe.com/go/flex2_devcenter

OnFlex.org

Weblog run by Ted Patrick, with frequent posts on Flex development issues:

http://www.onflex.org

Flex coders mailing list

Popular mailing list for discussing development using the Flex Framework:

http://tech.groups.yahoo.com/group/flexcoders/

Universal Desktop Weblog

Ryan Stewart's weblog, which focuses on the latest developments in the world of Rich Internet Applications:

http://blogs.zdnet.com/Stewart/

How to Contact Us

Please address comments and nontechnical questions concerning this book to the publisher:

O'Reilly Media, Inc.
1005 Gravenstein Highway North
Sebastopol, CA 95472
800-998-9938 (in the United States or Canada)
707-829-0515 (international or local)
707-829-0104 (fax)

We have a web page for this book, where we list errata, examples, and any additional information. You can access this page at:

http://www.oreilly.com/catalog/9780596513917

For more information about our books, conferences, Resource Centers, and the O'Reilly Network, see our web site at:

http://www.oreilly.com

About the Authors

Mike Chambers

Mike Chambers has spent the last eight years building applications that target the Flash runtime. During that time, he has worked with numerous technologies including Flash, Generator, .NET, Central, Flex, and Ajax. He is currently the senior product manager for developer relations for Apollo. He has written and spoken extensively on Flash and Rich Internet Application development and is coauthor of *Flash Enabled: Flash Design and Development for Devices* as well as *Generator and Flash Demystified*.

Mike received his Masters in International Economics and European Studies from the John Hopkins School of Advanced International Studies (SAIS) in 1998.

When he is not programming, Mike can be found playing Halo 2, trying to recover from his World of Warcraft addiction, or playing with his two daughters, Isabel and Aubrey.

Robert L. Dixon

Rob Dixon began developing Flash applications in 1998, back when Rich Internet Applications weren't nearly as well off. He is presently the Content Architect for the Platform Documentation group at Adobe. He developed sample applications and documentation for products including Apollo, ActionScript, Flash Player, and Central. He helped write *Programming ActionScript 3.0* and the *ActionScript Language Reference*.

In previous lives he programmed video games, designed web sites, built enterprise software using Java and .NET, and spoke at many software development conferences. He wrote a book on CASE software back when CASE was all the rage.

On weekends you can usually find him hiking or biking just generally cruising around in Marin County, California, if you know just where to look. Or if you attach a homing device to his jacket or something.

Jeff Swartz

Jeff Swartz first worked at Macromedia (now Adobe Systems) in 1992 and has participated in a number of multimedia and web software projects. He is currently the lead technical writer for the Apollo project. Jeff received a bachelor's degree in Computer Science and Mathematics from the University of Illinois at Urbana-Champaign in and studied at the Edinburgh University Department of Artificial Intelligence.

Audiences around the San Francisco Bay Area have tolerated Jeff's artistry on the trombone. He has served as Big Frank, a dancing hot dog, for Vienna Beef Ltd.

Acknowledgments

The authors would like to thank Mark Nichoson from Adobe and Steve Weiss, Phil Dangler, and Mary Brady from O'Reilly for helping make the book possible in an incredibly short amount of time.

Thank you to everyone on the Apollo team for all of the dedication and hard work in getting a 1.0 runtime out the door. Particular thanks to Chris Brichford, Ethan Malasky, Stan Switzer, and Oliver Goldman (all on the Apollo team) for reviewing and providing feedback on the book.

CHAPTER 1

Introduction to Apollo

Apollo is a new cross-platform desktop runtime being developed by Adobe that allows web developers to use web technologies to build and deploy Rich Internet Applications and web applications to the desktop.

In order to better understand what Apollo enables, and which problems it tries to address, it is useful to first take a quick look over at the (relatively short) history of web applications.

A Short History of Web Applications

Over the past couple of years, there has been an accelerating trend of applications moving from the desktop to the web browser. This has been driven by a number of factors, which include:

- The growth of the Internet as a communication medium
- The relative ease of deployment of web applications
- The ability to target multiple operating systems via the browser
- The maturity of higher-level client technologies, such the browser and the Flash Player runtime

Early web applications were built primarily with HTML and JavaScript, which, for the most part, heavily relied on client/server interactions and page refreshes. This page refresh model was consistent with the document-based metaphor for which the browser was originally designed, but provided a relatively poor user experience when displaying applications.

However, with the maturation of the Flash Player runtime, and more recently Ajax-type functionality in the browser, it became possible for developers to begin breaking away from page-based application flows. In short, developers began to be able to offer richer application experiences via the browser. In a whitepaper from March 2002, Macromedia coined the term Rich Internet Application (RIA), to describe these new types of applications in browsers, which "blend content, application logic and communications...to make the Internet more usable and enjoyable." These applications provided richer, more desktop-like experiences, while still retaining the core cross-platform nature of the Web:

> Internet applications are all about reach. The promise of the web is one of content and applications anywhere, regardless of the platform or device. Rich clients must embrace and support all popular desktop operating systems, as well as the broadest range of emerging device platforms such as smart phones, PDAs, set-top boxes, game consoles, and Internet appliances.

TIP

You can find the complete whitepaper and more information on RIAs at: *http://download.macromedia.com/pub/flash/whitepapers/richclient.pdf*

The paper goes on to list some features that define RIAs:

- Provide an efficient, high performance runtime for executing code, content, and communications.
- Integrate content, communications, and application interfaces into a common environment.
- Provide powerful and extensible object models for interactivity.
- Enable rapid application development through components and re-use.

- Enable the use of web and data services provided by application servers.
- Embrace connected and disconnected clients.
- Enable easy deployment on multiple platforms and devices.

This movement toward providing richer, more desktop-like application experiences in the browser (enabled by the Flash Player runtime, and more recently by Ajax techniques) has led to an explosion of web applications.

Today the web has firmly established itself as an application deployment platform that offers benefits to both developers and end users. These benefits include the ability to:

- Target multiple platforms and operating systems.
- Develop with relatively high-level programming and layout languages.
- Allow end users to access their applications and data from virtually any Internet-connected computer.

The growth of web applications can be seen in both the Web 2.0 movement, which consists almost entirely of web based applications and APIs, as well as the adoption of web applications as a core business model of major companies and organizations.

Problems with Delivering Applications via the Browser

As web applications have become more complex, they have begun to push the boundaries of both the capabilities of the browser and the usability of the application. As their popularity grows, these issues become more apparent and important and highlight that there are still a number of significant issues for both developers and end users when deploying applications via the browser.

The web browser was original designed to deliver and display HTML-based documents. Indeed, the basic design of the browser has not significantly shifted from this purpose. This fundamental conflict between document- and application-focused functionality creates a number of problems when deploying applications via the browser.

Conflicting UI

Applications deployed via the browser have their own user interface, which often conflicts with the user interface of the browser. This application within an application model often results in user interfaces that conflict with and contradict each other. This can lead to user confusion in the best cases, and application failure in the worst cases. The classic example of this is the browser's Back button. The Back button makes sense when browsing documents, but it does not always make sense in the context of an application. Although there are a number of solutions that attempt to solve this problem, they are applied to applications inconsistently; users may not know whether a specific application supports the Back button, or whether it will force their application to unload, causing it to lose its state and data.

Distance from the Desktop

Due in part to the web security model (which restricts access to the users machine), applications that run in the browser often do not support the type of user interactions with the operating system that users expect from applications. For example, you cannot drag a file into a browser-based application and have the application act on that file. Nor can the web application interact with other applications on the user's computer.

RIAs have tried to improve on this by making richer, more desktop-like interfaces possible in the browser, but they have not been able to overcome the fundamental limitations and separation of the browser from the desktop.

Primarily Online Experience

Because web applications are delivered from a server and do not reside on the users machine, web applications are a primarily online experience. While there are attempts underway to make offline web-based applications possible, they do not provide a consistent development model, they fail to work across different browsers, and they often require the user to interact with and manage their application and browser in complex and unexpected ways.

Lowest Common Denominator

Finally, as applications become richer and more complex and begin to push the boundaries of JavaScript and DHTML, developers are increasingly faced with differences in browser functionality and APIs. While these issues can often be overcome with browser-specific code, it leads to code that is more difficult to maintain and scale, and takes time away from function-driven development.

While JavaScript frameworks are a popular way to help address these issues, they can offer only the functionality provided by the browser, and often resort to the lowest common denominator of features between browsers to ease the development model. While this issue doesn't affect Flash-based RIAs, the end result for JavaScript- or DHTML-based applications is a lowest common denominator user experience and interaction model, as well as increased development, testing, and deployment costs for the developer.

The fact that web applications have flourished despite these drawbacks is a testament to the attractiveness of having a platform with a good development model that has the ability to deliver applications to multiple operating systems. A platform that offered the reach and development model of the browser, while providing the functionality and richness of a desktop application, would provide the best of both worlds. This is what Apollo aims to do.

Introducing the Apollo Runtime

So, what is Apollo, and how can it make web application development and deployment better?

Apollo is the code name for a new cross-operating system runtime being developed by Adobe that allows web developers to leverage their existing web development skills (such as Flash, Flex, HTML, JavaScript, and PDF) to build and deploy Rich Internet Applications and content to the desktop.

In essence, it provides a platform in between the desktop and the browser, which combines the reach and ease of development of the web model with the functionality and richness of the desktop model.

NOTE

Apollo is the code name for the project. The final name had not yet been announced at the time of this writing.

It is important to step back for a second and point out what Apollo is not. Apollo is not a general desktop runtime meant to compete with lower-level application runtimes. This means that you probably wouldn't want to build Photoshop on top of Apollo. Apollo's primary use case is enabling Rich Internet and web applications to be deployed to the desktop. This is a very important but subtle distinction, as enabling RIAs on the desktop is the primary use case driving the Apollo 1.0 feature set.

At its core, Apollo is built on top of web technologies, which allow web developers to develop for and deploy to the desktop using the same technologies and development models that they use today when deploying applications on the Web.

Primary Apollo Technologies

There are three primary technologies included within Apollo, which fall into two distinct categories: application technologies and document technologies.

Primary Application Technologies

Application technologies are technologies that can be used as the basis of an application within Apollo. Apollo contains two primary application technologies, Flash and HTML, both of which can be used on their own to build and deploy Apollo applications.

Flash

One of the core technologies Apollo is built on is the Flash Player. Specifically, Apollo is built on top of Flash Player 9, which includes the ECMAScript-based ActionScript 3 as well as the open source Tamarin virtual machine (which will be used to interpret JavaScript in future versions of Firefox).

TIP

You can find more information on the open source Tamarin project at on the Mozilla website site at *http://www.mozilla.org/projects/tamarin/*.

Not only are all of the existing Flash Player APIs available within Apollo, but some of those APIs have also been expanded and/or enhanced. Some of the functionality that the Flash Player provides to Apollo includes:

- Just-in-time Interpreted ActionScript engine for speedy application performance
- Full networking stack, including HTTP and RTMP, as well as Binary and XML sockets

- Complete vector-based rendering engine and drawing APIs
- Extensive multimedia support including bitmaps, vectors, audio, and video

Of course, the Flex 2 framework is built on top of ActionScript 3, which means that you can also take advantage of all of the features and functionality that Flex offers in order to build Apollo applications.

HTML

The second application technology within Apollo is HTML. This is a full HTML rendering engine, which includes support for:

- HTML
- JavaScript
- CSS
- XHTML
- Document Object Model (DOM)

Yes, you read that right. You don't have to use Flash to build Apollo applications. You can build a full-featured application using just HTML and JavaScript. This usually surprises some developers who expect Apollo to focus only on Flash. However, at its core, Apollo is a runtime targeted at web developers using web technologies—and what is more of a web technology than HTML and JavaScript?

The HTML engine used within Apollo is the open source WebKit engine. This is the engine behind a number of browsers, including KHTML on KDE and Safari on Mac OS X.

TIP

You can find more information on the WebKit open source project at *http://www.webkit.org*.

Why WebKit? Adobe spent a considerable amount of time researching which HTML engine to use within Apollo and used a number of criteria that ultimately led them to settle on WebKit.

Open project. Adobe knew from the very beginning that it did not want to create and maintain its own HTML rendering engine. Not only would this be an immense amount of work, but it would also make it difficult for developers, who would then have to become familiar with all of the quirks of yet another HTML engine.

WebKit provides Apollo with a full-featured HTML engine that is under continuous development by a robust development community that includes individual developers as well as large companies such as Nokia and Apple. This allows Adobe to focus on bug fixes and features, and also means that Adobe can actively contribute back to WebKit, while also taking advantage of the contributions made by other members of the WebKit project.

Proven technology that web developers know. As discussed earlier, one of the biggest problems with complex web development is ensuring that content works consistently across browsers. While something may work perfectly in Firefox on the Mac, it may completely fail in Internet Explorer on Windows. Because of this, testing and debugging browser-based content can be a nightmare for developers.

Adobe wanted to ensure that developers were already familiar with the HTML engine used within Apollo, and that they did not have to learn new all of the quirks and bugs of a new engine. Since Safari (which is built on top of WebKit) is the default browser for Mac OS X, developers should be familiar with developing for it.

Minimum effect on Apollo runtime size. The target size for Apollo is between 5 and 9 MB. The WebKit code base was well-written and organized and had a minimal impact on the final Apollo runtime size. Indeed, the current runtime size with both Flash and HTML is just a little over 5 MB.

Proven ability to run on mobile devices. While the first release of Apollo runs only on personal computers, the long-term vision is to extend the Apollo runtime from the desktop to cell phones and other devices. WebKit has a proven ability to run on such devices and has been ported to cell phones by both Nokia and Apple.

Primary Document Technology

Document technologies within Apollo refer to technologies whose primary purpose is for the rendering and interaction with electronic documents.

PDF and HTML are the primary document technologies available within Apollo.

PDF

PDF functionality is not included in Alpha 1 of Apollo, so we cannot go into too much detail of how it is implemented. However, in general Apollo applications, both Flash- and HTML-based, will be able to leverage and interact with PDF content.

HTML

HTML was originally designed as a document technology, and today it provides rich and robust control over content and text layout and styling. HTML can be used as a document technology within Apollo—both within an existing HTML application as well as within a Flash-based application.

What Does An Apollo Application Contain?

Now that we know what technologies are available to applications running on top of the Apollo runtime (see Figure 1-1), let's look at how those technologies can be combined to build an Apollo application.

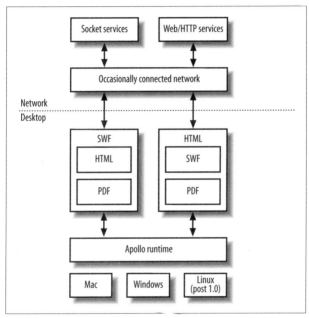

Figure 1-1. Apollo application structure

Applications can consist of the following combinations of technologies:

- Flash only (including Flex)
- Flash-based with HTML content
- HTML/JavaScript only
- HTML/JavaScript-based with Flash content
- All combinations can also leverage PDF content

Technology Integration and Script Bridging

Because WebKit and the Flash Player are both included within the runtime, they are integrated together on a very low level. For example, when HTML is included within Flash content, it is actually rendered via the Flash display pipeline, which, among other things, means that anything that you can do to a bitmap within Flash (blur, rotate, transform, etc.) can also be done to HTML.

This low-level integration also applies to the script engines within Apollo (that run ActionScript and JavaScript). Apollo provides script bridging between the two languages and environments, which makes the following possible:

- JavaScript code to call ActionScript APIs
- ActionScript code to call JavaScript APIs
- ActionScript code to directly manipulate the HTML DOM
- Event registration both ways between JavaScript and ActionScript

Note that the script bridging is "pass by reference." So when passing an object instance from ActionScript to JavaScript (or vice versa), changes to that instance in one environment will affect the instance in the other environment. Among other things, this makes it possible to maintain a reference to HTML nodes from within ActionScript and modify them, or to register and listen for events.

This low-level script bridging between the two environments makes it very easy for developers to create applications that are a combination of both HTML and Flash.

TIP

Script Bridging is covered in more detail in Chapter 4.

The end result of all of this is that if you are a web developer, then you already have all of the skills necessary to build an Apollo application.

Apollo Functionality

If Apollo did not provide additional functionality and APIs and simply allowed web applications to run on the desktop, it would not be at all compelling. Fortunately, Apollo provides a rich set of programming APIs, as well as close integration with the desktop that allows developers to build applications that take advantage of the fact that they're running on the user's desktop.

Apollo Programming APIs

In addition to all of the functionality and APIs already offered by the Flash Player and WebKit engine, Apollo provides additional functionality and APIs.

TIP

Apollo APIs will be exposed to both ActionScript and JavaScript.

Some of the new functionality includes, but is not limited to:

- Complete file I/O API
- Complete native windowing API
- Complete native menuing API
- Online/Offline APIs to detect when network connectivity has changed
- Data Caching and Syncing APIs to make it easier to develop applications that work on- and offline.
- Complete control over application chrome
- Local storage/settings APIs
- System notification APIs (that tie into OS-specific notification mechanisms)
- Application update APIs

Note that functionality may be implemented directly within the Apollo runtime or on the framework layer (in Flex and JavaScript), or by using a combination of both.

Apollo Desktop Integration

As discussed earlier, applications deployed via the browser cannot always support the same user interactions as desktop applications. This leads to applications that can be cumbersome for the user to interact with, as they do not allow the type of application interactions with which users are familiar.

Because an Apollo application is a desktop application, it is able to provide the type of application interactions and experience that users expect from an application. This functionality includes, but is not limited to:

- Appropriate install/uninstall rituals
- Desktop install touchpoints (i.e., shortcuts, etc.)
- Rich drag-and-drop support:
    Between operating system and Apollo applications
    Between Apollo applications
    Between native applications and Apollo applications
- Rich clipboard support
- System notifications
- Icons
- Ability for applications to run in the background

Once installed, an Apollo application is just another native application, which means that the operating system and users can interact with it as it does with any other application. For example, things such as OS-level application prefetching and switching work the same with Apollo applications as they do with native applications.

The goal is that the end user doesn't know they are running an application that leverages Apollo. He should be able to interact with an Apollo application in the same way that he interacts with any other application running on his desktop.

Apollo Development Toolset

One of the reasons web applications have been successful is that they allow developers to easily deploy applications that users can run regardless of which OS they are on. Whether Mac, Windows, Linux, Solaris, or cell phones, web applications provide reach.

However, success is based not only on cross-platform deployment, but also on the cross-platform nature of the development environment. This ensures that any developer can develop for—and leverage—the technology. Neither the runtime nor the development tools are tied to a specific OS.

The same is true of Apollo. Not only does Apollo provide the cross-platform reach of web applications, but, just as importantly, Apollo applications can be developed and packaged on virtually any operating system.

In fact, Apollo itself does not have a compiler or specialized IDE. Apollo applications just consist of web content, such as Flash and HTML. Any tool that can edit an HTML or JavaScript file can also be used to create an Apollo application.

TIP

A beta version of Flex Builder with Apollo support is included with the Apollo Alpha.

Because Apollo applications are built with existing web technologies such as HTML and Flash, you can use the same tools that you use to create browser-based content to create Apollo applications. The Apollo SDK provides a number of free command-line tools that make it possible to test, debug, and package Apollo applications with virtually any web development and design tool.

ADL	Allows Apollo applications to be run without having to first install them
ADT	Packages Apollo applications into distributable installation packages

While Adobe will be adding support to its own web development and design tools for authoring Apollo content, they are not required. Using the Apollo command-line tools, you can create an Apollo application with any web development tool. You can use the same web development and design tools that you are already using today.

TIP

The Development Workflow will be covered in depth in Chapter 2.

Is Apollo the End of Web Applications in the Browser?

So, by this point, you may be saying to yourself, "Gee, Apollo sure sounds great! Why would anyone ever want to deploy an application to the browser again? Is Apollo the end of web applications within the browser?"

No.

Let's repeat that again: no.

Apollo solves most of the problems with deploying web applications via the browser. However, there are still advantages to deploying applications via the browser. The fact that there are so many web applications despite the disadvantages discussed earlier is a testament to the advantages of running within the browser. When those advantages outweigh the disadvantages, developers will still deploy their applications via the web browser.

But is it not necessarily an either/or question. Because Apollo applications are built using web technologies, the application that you deploy via the web browser can be quickly turned into an Apollo application. You can have a web-based version that provides the browser-based functionality, and then also have an Apollo-based version that takes advantage of running on the desktop. Both versions could leverage the same technologies, languages, and code base.

Apollo applications complement web applications. They do not replace them.

CHAPTER 2

Getting Started with Apollo Development

This chapter discusses how to set up your development environment and start building Apollo applications using the Flex framework. It covers:

- Where to get the tools and resources you need to develop Apollo applications
- How to set up your development environment
- How to develop, test, and deploy a simple Hello World application

This chapter has complete information on how to compile, test, package, and distribute Apollo applications.

Installing the Apollo Alpha 1 Runtime

You will need to install the Apollo Alpha 1 runtime on your computer and any computers on which you want to run your Apollo applications. The Apollo Alpha 1 installer is available on the Adobe web site at:

http://www.adobe.com/go/apollo

Windows Installation

To install the Apollo runtime on a Windows computer:

1. Download the Apollo Runtime Alpha 1 Windows installer file from *http://www.adobe.com/go/apollo*.
2. Open the ZIP file.

3. Double-click the *Apollo.msi* file.

   An installation window is displayed.

4. When the installation is complete, click the OK button.

Mac OS Installation

To install the Apollo runtime on Mac OS:

1. Download the Apollo Runtime Alpha 1 Mac installer file from *http://www.adobe.com/go/apollo*.

2. Open the zip file and double-click the *Adobe Apollo.dmg* file.

   The Adobe Apollo window is displayed.

3. Double-click the *Adobe Apollo.pkg* file.

   The Install Adobe Apollo window is displayed.

4. Click the Continue button, in the lower lefthand corner of the window.

   The "Select a Destination" page of the installer is displayed.

5. Select the destination volume and click the Continue button.

   The Easy Install button is displayed.

6. Click the Install button, in the lower lefthand corner of the window.

7. After the installation is completed, click the Close button, in the lower righthand corner of the installation window.

What You Need in Order to Develop Apollo Applications

You will need to install the Apollo Alpha 1 runtime on your computer and on any computers. (See the previous section.)

To develop Flex-based Apollo applications, you will need one of the following sets of tools:

Adobe Flex Builder 2.0.1 and the Apollo Extensions for Flex Builder 2.0.1

> Flex Builder 2.0.1 provides a full IDE for developing and debugging Flex applications.
>
> The Apollo Extensions for Flex Builder 2.0.1 provide capabilities for developing, debugging, and packaging Apollo applications within Flex Builder 2.0.1. It includes support for the Apollo API. It also includes the tools and resources in the Apollo SDK. You can obtain the Apollo Extensions for Flex Builder 2.0.1 from *http://www.adobe. com/go/apollo*.

The Apollo SDK

> The Apollo SDK is free for download from Adobe. While it does not include the visual layout and debugging features available in Flex Builder 2.0.1, it does include a full-featured Flex command-line compiler.
>
> The Apollo SDK includes tools for developing, debugging, and packaging Apollo applications.
>
> You can download the Apollo SDK from *http://www. adobe.com/go/apollo*.

Downloading and Setting Up Flex Builder 2.0.1 and Apollo Extensions

A trial version of Flex Builder 2.0.1 is available at the adobe. com web site:

> *http://www.adobe.com/products/flex/flexbuilder/*

Beta versions of the Apollo Extensions for Flex Builder 2.0.1 are available from the Adobe web site at:

> *http://www.adobe.com/go/apollo*

These extensions to Flex Builder add support for creating, developing, debugging, and deploying Apollo applications from within Flex Builder.

To install and configure the Flex Builder Apollo Extensions:

1. Install Flex Builder 2.0.1 (either standalone or Eclipse Plug-in version).

2. Run the Flex Builder Apollo Extensions installer. Accept the license agreement and, when prompted, navigate to the directory containing Flex Builder 2.0.1.

Downloading and Setting Up the Apollo SDK

If you do *not* use Flex Builder 2.0.1, you need to install the Apollo SDK, both of which are available for free at the Adobe web site:

> *http://www.adobe.com/go/apollo*

You will also need to have a Java runtime environment or Java Developers Kit installed on your system. If you do not already have Java installed and configured on your system, you can download it from:

> *http://java.sun.com/j2se/1.4.2/download.html*

Follow the directions included with Java to install and configure it.

The Apollo SDK includes the following resources:

Item	Description
ADL	This is used to launch and test an Apollo application without having to first install it.
ADT	This is used to to package an Apollo application for distribution.
apolloframework.swc and *apolloglobal.swc* files	These are libraries containing Apollo core and Framework classes that the MXMLC compiler uses when you compile a SWF file for use in an Apollo application.
The *application.xml* file	A sample application descriptor file, used to provide settings for an application.
The *application.xsd* file	The XML schema for the *application.xml* file.

Installation and Configuration on Mac OS

On Mac OS, follow these steps:

1. Download the *apollo_sdk.zip* file to your desktop.

2. Create an *Apollo_SDK* subdirectory in the */Applications* directory (the *Applications* directory at the root of the system). You place the SDK in a different path, but make sure to adjust the path when following the following instructions.

3. Double-click the ZIP file and copy the contents to the *Apollo_SDK* directory. (For example, the *.bin* file should go in the root of the *Apollo_SDK* directory.)

4. Open the */Applications/Apollo_SDK/runtime* directory and double-click the *Adobe Apollo.dmg* file.

5. Drag the *Adobe Apollo.framework* folder contained in the DMG file to the */Applications/Apollo_SDK/runtime* directory (in the Finder).

   This installs the Apollo runtime used by ADL.

6. The next step is to ensure that the Apollo command-line tools are added to the system's path. This ensures that they can be run from any directory. In the Mac OS Terminal application, open a *new* window.

   The terminal session should open to your user directory. If not, navigate to it.

7. Type:

   ```
   open c .profile
   ```

   The *.profile* file opens in the system text editor.

8. Add this line to the end of the file:

   ```
   export PATH=$PATH:/Applications/Apollo_SDK/bin/
   ```

   If a PATH is already set in your file, add the Apollo SDK path to it.

9. Save the file.

10. In the Mac OS Terminal application, type:

    ```
    source .profile
    ```

    This causes the chnages to take effect.

Installation and Configuration on Windows

On Windows, follow these steps carefully:

1. Download the Apollo SDK ZIP file.

2. Open the *apollo_sdk.zip* file and then extract its contents to *C:\Program Files\ apollo_sdk*.

3. Open the System Properties dialog box and click the Advanced tab. This can be found in the System setting in the Control Panel.

4. Click the Environment Variables button.

5. Select the PATH entry and then click the Edit button. Add the path to the *bin* directory to the end of the current variable value:

   ```
   ; C:\Program Files\Apollo_SDK\bin\
   ```

Building a Sample Apollo Application

The Apollo development process can be summarized in four steps:

1. Create the application descriptor file.

2. Design and program the application.

3. Test and debug the application.

4. Package the application for distribution.

This chapter walks you through these steps using a very simple Hello World example. Following these steps will help you verify that your Apollo development environment is working. When you are done, you will have written a complete Apollo application, and can be sure that your development environment is set up and configured correctly.

From building this simple application, you should learn the following:

• How to write basic MXML code for an Apollo application

- How to test and debug the application
- How to package the application into a distributable AIR file, which can be distributed to users for installation on their computers

The steps for building and debugging are different depending on whether you are using the Flex Builder tool or the Apollo SDK, so there are separate sections for each of these tools.

Ideas for creating more interesting Apollo applications are provided in Chapters 3 and 5.

Building and Debugging the Hello World Application in Flex Builder 2.0.1

If you have not installed Flex Builder 2.0.1 and are using the Apollo SDK, skip ahead to "Building and Debugging the Hello World Application Using the Apollo SDK."

Creating an Apollo application in Flex Builder 2.0.1 is similar to creating a Flex application for the Web. To get started, follow these steps:

1. Open Flex Builder 2.0.1.
2. Select File → New (Control-N on Windows or ⌘-N on a Mac).

   The New dialog box is displayed.
3. Expand the Flex folder and select Apollo Project. Then click the Next button.

   The New Apollo Project dialog box (Figure 2-1) is displayed.
4. Leave the Basic option selected and click the Next button.
5. In the next page of the dialog box, type **HelloWorld** as the Project Name and leave the Use Default Location option selected. Then click the Next button.

   Do *not* click the Finish button yet.

Figure 2-1. The New Apollo Project dialog box

6. In the next page of the dialog box (for setting build paths), make no changes and click the Next button.

   Do *not* click the Finish button yet.

   The Application XML Properties panel is displayed.

7. Specify the following settings for the Apollo application:

Field	Enter this
ID	com.oreilly.apollo.gettingStarted.HelloWorld
Name	Hello World
Publisher	Your name
Description	A sample Apollo application
Copyright	©Your name. All rights reserved.

The ID field should contain a value that uniquely identifies your application. To make sure it is unique, many people begin the ID with the address of a domain that they own (such as com.oreilly.apollo in the preceding example).

The Name field defines the application name that is displayed to users. The Publisher, Description, and Copyright values are optional; they are displayed in the application installer.

The values entered in the Application XML panel will be saved in the application descriptor file, under the name *HelloWorld-app.xml*.

8. Finally, click the Finish button at the bottom of the dialog box.

Now that the Apollo project has been set up, you can write the MXML code for this application:

1. Edit the file *HelloWorld.mxml* (which should already be open in the Flex Builder editor panel). It should currently look something like this:

   ```
   <?xml version="1.0" encoding="utf-8"?>
   <mx:ApolloApplication xmlns:mx="http://www.adobe.com/
   2006/mxml"
     layout="absolute">

   </mx:ApolloApplication>
   ```

   Now modify that code so it matches the following:

   ```
   <?xml version="1.0" encoding="utf-8"?>
   <mx:ApolloApplication xmlns:mx="http://www.adobe.com/
   2006/mxml"
     layout="absolute"
     title="Hello World"
     backgroundColor="0xFFCC00">

     <mx:Label text="Hello Apollo"
       fontSize="18"
       horizontalCenter="0"
       verticalCenter="0"/>

   </mx:ApolloApplication>
   ```

The main changes you made were to:

- Define `title` and `backgroundColor` attributes of the ApolloApplication component, as shown in the code.
- Add a Label component and define its `text`, `horizontalCenter`, and `verticalCenter` attributes.

2. Save the file.

   Now you can test the application.

3. Click the Debug button, or select Run → Debug to debug the application.

   The resulting application should look similar to Figure 2-2 (with the exact chrome depending on the system you are developing on).

Figure 2-2. Hello World

4. Flex Builder 2.0.1 reports any errors in the Console panel. If you experience errors, make sure that you have carefully followed the steps in this tutorial.

5. You can set breakpoints and use Flex Builder's debugging tools just as you can when debugging any other Flex 2.0 application.

Now the application is ready to be packaged for distribution. Skip ahead to "Packaging and Distributing the Hello World Application."

Building and Debugging the Hello World Application Using the Apollo SDK

If you have installed Flex Builder 2.0.1 and followed the previous instructions, you can skip this section.

In this tutorial, you will create the source files for the Apollo application and then test the application using the Apollo SDK command-line compiler.

Before starting, make sure that you have installed the Apollo SDK, and that you have configured your system to work with these tools.

First, create a project directory. This directory will contain all of the source files for the project.

Next, create the application descriptor file, which is also referred to as the application XML file:

1. Open a text editor application, and type the following in a new file:

```xml
<?xml version="1.0" encoding="UTF-8"?>
<application xmlns="http://ns.adobe.com/apollo/
application/1.0.M3" appId="com.oreilly.apollo.
gettingStarted.HelloWorld" version="1.0">
  <properties>
    <name>Hello World</name>
    <publisher>Your name </publisher>
    <description>A sample Apollo application.
    </description>
    <copyright>(C) 2007 Your name  All rights reserved.
  </copyright>
  </properties>
  <rootContent systemChrome="standard"
    transparent="false">
    HelloWorld.swf
  </rootContent>
</application>
```

These are the most important settings in this file:

- The `appId` attribute value should uniquely identify your application. To make sure it is unique, many people begin the ID with the address of a domain that they own (such as `com.oreilly.apollo` in the preceding example).

- The `name` attribute defines the application name that is displayed to users.

- The `publisher`, `description`, and `copyright` values are optional. They will be displayed in the installer interface when a user installs your application.

- The `rootContent` element identifies the SWF file that will be the root of the application. (You will compile this SWF file soon.)

- The `systemChrome` attribute is set to `"standard"`. This means that the application will use *system chrome*, the standard set of user interface elements defined by the operating system for a normal application window. These elements include borders, a title bar, maximize and minimize buttons, and a close button. You can also suppress the system chrome by setting this attribute to `"none"` and then defining your own *custom chrome* for the application window. For more information, see "Making a Window Transparent" and "Using Your Own Window Chrome Elements" in Chapter 5.

- The `transparent` attribute is set to `false`. This means that the application's background will be opaque rather than transparent. For more information about using window transparency see "Making a Window Transparent" in Chapter 5.

2. Save the file to your project directory and give it the name *HelloWorld-app.xml*.

Next you will create the MXML code for this application:

1. Create a new file in the text editor application.

2. Add the following to the file:

```
<?xml version="1.0" encoding="utf-8"?>
<mx:ApolloApplication xmlns:mx="http://www.adobe.com/
2006/mxml"
  layout="absolute"
  title="Hello World"
  backgroundColor="0xFFCC00">

  <mx:Label text="Hello Apollo"
    fontSize="18"
    horizontalCenter="0"
    verticalCenter="0"/>

</mx:ApolloApplication>
```

This defines the MXML source code for the application:

- The ApolloApplication component is a subclass of the Flex 2 Application component. It defines the main window of the application. The value of the title attribute will appear in the title bar of the main window.

- The Label component is used to display the simple text message "Hello Apollo".

3. Save the file with the name *HelloWorld.mxml*.

Next, you can compile the SWF file, using the amxmlc command-line tool: the amxmlc utility calls the MXMLC compiler with options that tell it to use the Apollo libraries.

1. Open the Terminal application in Mac OS or the Command Prompt in Windows.

2. Use the cd command to navigate to the project directory that you set up for this Hello World project.

3. Type the following command line, and then press the Enter key:

```
amxmlc HelloWorld.mxml
```

4. If no errors are generated, the compiler generates the *HelloWorld.swf* file in the project directory.

Now you can test the application, using the ADL command-line tool:

1. Type the following in the command-line window:

   ```
   adl application.xml
   ```

2. If no errors are generated, the Hello World application (Figure 2-3) opens.

Figure 2-3. Hello World

Packaging and Distributing the Hello World Application

Apollo applications packaged into an AIR file, which is an installer file that contains the application's root SWF file, its application descriptor file, and any other assets such as images or HTML files that should be installed with the application.

Users who have already obtained the Apollo runtime can double-click an AIR file to install your Apollo application on their machine.

Flex Builder 2.0.1 includes commands for automatically packaging your application as an AIR file.

If you are using the Apollo SDK to compile your application, you can use the Apollo Developer Tool (ADT) to create the packaged AIR file.

Packaging the application using Flex Builder 2.0.1

1. Make sure the Hello World project is open in Flex Builder.

2. Select File → Export from the main Flex Builder menu.

   Flex Builder displays the Export dialog box.

3. Select the entry named Deployable AIR File and then click the Next button.

   The next panel is the AIR Deployment Export Wizard, as shown in Figure 2-4.

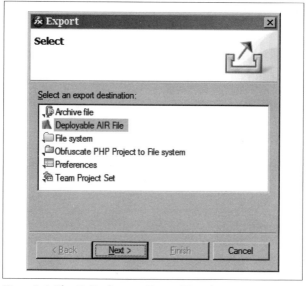

Figure 2-4. The Air Deployment Export Wizard

1. Find and select the *HelloWorld-app.xml* file in the list, and then click the Next button. Figure 2-5 shows a screenshot of this panel.

Figure 2-5. Select the file for export

2. In the next panel, you could select any auxiliary assets (such as SWF files, HTML files, or media files) that you want to include with the Apollo application. However, the Hello World application includes no such assets.

   You could also change the destination for the AIR file that will be created, but for this example you should keep the default destination. Figure 2-6 shows a screenshot of this panel.

3. Click the Finish button to generate the AIR file.

4. Test the generated AIR file by launching it from your operating system to see if the Hello World application installs correctly.

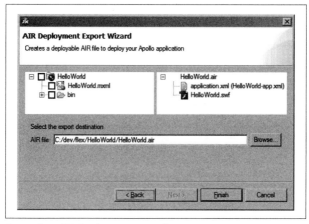

Figure 2-6. AIR Deployment Wizard

Packaging the application using ADT

If you do not use Flex Builder 2.0.1, you will need to use the ADT tool (Figure 2-6) to package the Apollo application into an AIR file.

1. Open the Terminal application in Mac OS or the Command Prompt in Windows.

2. Use the `cd` command to navigate to the project directory that you set up for this Hello World project.

3. Type the following (on one line) and press the Enter key:

   ```
   adt -package HelloWorld.air HelloWorld-app.xml
   HelloWorld.swf
   ```

   The ADT tool creates the *HelloWorld.air* file in the project directory.

4. Test the generated AIR file by launching it from your operating system to see if the Hello World application installs correctly.

Distributing and installing your application

You can distribute your Apollo application by distributing the AIR file for that application.

Users will need to install the Apollo runtime (available at *http://www.adobe.com/go/apollo*). Then they can run the AIR file to launch the Apollo installer for your application.

TIP

In a future build, you will be able to also create native installers that can first check for and install the Apollo runtime, before installing the application.

Next Steps

Now that your Apollo development environment is set up and you are able to create, package, and run the HelloWorld sample, it's time to learn more about the power of Apollo. The next chapters will present the details of some of Apollo's most powerful features.

TIP

If you plan on delivering your Apollo application via a link in a web page, be sure to associate the AIR MIME type in your web server. For example, in the Apache HTTP Server, you typically will add the following line to the httpd.conf file:

```
AddType application/vnd.adobe.apollo-install-
package .air
```

CHAPTER 3

Using HTML Within Flex-Based Apollo Applications

Apollo gives developers a brand new way to integrate HTML rendering into desktop applications. Apollo's new HTML functionality includes the ability to:

- Load and render complete web pages (HTML and XHTML) from local and remote URLs as well as a string.

- Access and manipulate the full Document Object Model (DOM).

- Call JavaScript functions and reference JavaScript objects from within your ActionScript code, and vice versa.

- Arrange the Flex HTML component in your application interface as you would any other Flex UI component.

- Graphically alter the HTMLControl object or Flex HTML component as you would any Sprite or DisplayObject in ActionScript.

The new flash.html.HTMLControl class handles the core HTML loading, rendering, and script execution duties. Based on the HTMLControl class, the new Flex HTML component integrates the same HTML rendering power into the Flex UI framework.

An application with simple HTML rendering or web browsing needs can use the Flex HTML component with little or no ActionScript coding. Of course, more complex requirements will call for additional coding in either ActionScript or JavaScript.

This chapter describes Apollo's HTML capabilities and offers a number of quick examples to get you started writing HTML-enabled Apollo applications.

You can also refer to the "Working with HTML" section of Chapter 5 for more ways to use HTML in Apollo.

HTML Support in Apollo

The Apollo HTMLControl class uses WebKit (*www.webkit.org*) as its HTML rendering engine. WebKit is an open source web browser engine that was originally used in the Safari browser.

The Apollo HTMLControl class can render standard HTML 4 or XHTML content. It provides complete support for the CSS 1.0 standard, and nearly complete support for CSS 2.1 and CSS 3. The Document Object Model (DOM) supports the W3C DOM Level 2 standard (*www.w3.org/DOM*).

The HTMLControl class also provides full support for the Java-Script language, based on the ECMAScript 3 standard. Now your Flex, Flash, and ActionScript applications can use Java-Script methods and properties to offer AJAX-style page inter-action and even better user experiences.

The HTMLControl class even supports embedded SWF files, meaning you could run a Flash or Flex application within an HTMLControl object in Apollo applications, although this feature is not available in the public Alpha.

Neither the Apollo HTMLControl class nor the Flex HTML component has all the features of a complete web browser. However, you could use either one to build your own customized web browser applications.

TIP

The HTML functionality within Apollo Alpha 1 is only partially implemented. Additional functionality, APIs, and events are being developed.

The HTMLControl class and the Flex HTML Component

The new `flash.html.HTMLControl` class provides the methods and properties that retrieve, load, and render HTML content. The `HTMLControl` class is a subclass of the `flash.display.DisplayObject` class, so it can be manipulated in the display list like any other `DisplayObject` instance.

The Flex `HTML` component presents the `HTMLControl` class as a UIComponent, giving it all the benefits of the Flex UI framework.

The following table lists the functional similarities and differences between the Flex `HTML` component and the `HTMLControl` class.

Capabilities	Flex HTML component	HTMLControl class
Superclass	`mx.core.ScrollControlBase`	`flash.display.Sprite`
Load HTML from a URL	Set the `location` property	Call the `load( )` method
Load HTML from a String	Set the `htmlText` property	Call the `loadString( )` method
Access or manipulate the DOM	Use the `javascriptWindow` or `javascriptDocument` properties	Use the `window` or `window.document` properties
Events dispatched	<ul><li>`locationChange`</li><li>`htmlTextChanged`</li><li>`domInitialize`</li><li>`htmlRender`</li><li>`complete`</li></ul>	<ul><li>`domInitialize`</li><li>`complete`</li><li>`htmlBoundsChange`</li><li>`htmlRender`</li><li>`scroll`</li></ul>
Other capabilities	<ul><li>Can be used in Flex layouts with no extra coding</li><li>Component can be styled using CSS</li><li>Can be used as an item renderer</li><li>Provides scrollbars</li></ul>	<ul><li>Can listen for changes to bounds of rendered HTML</li><li>Can control scroll position</li><li>Does not provide scrollbars</li></ul>

Using the Flex HTML Component

The Flex HTML component offers full HTML support, easy integration into a Flex application, and a programming interface similar to other Flex components.

The HTML component can be declared in MXML like any other Flex component. Here's an example that sets the HTML component to stretch to fit the height and width of the window:

```
<mx:HTML id="html" width="100%" height="100%" />
```

Navigating to a Web Page

You can tell the HTML component which web page to load by setting its location property to a valid URL string. The following example sets the HTML instance declared above to a specific URL value:

```
html.location = "http://www.adobe.com";
```

The URL string should contain the initial URL scheme portion of the URL, such as "http://".

The following table shows the URL schemes that the HTMLControl class currently supports. These include some standard protocols, plus three new protocols that specify files found in common directory locations known to the Apollo application:

Protocol string	Description
http:	Identifies a web resource to load using the standard HyperText Transfer Protocol.
https:	Identifies a web resource to load using the Transport Layer Security (TLS) or Secure Sockets Layer (SSL) secure communication protocols.
file:	Specifies a file to load from the local file system.
app-storage:	Identifies a file to load from the application storage directory.
app-resource:	Identifies a file to load from this application's installation folder.

For more information about the URI schemes for common directory locations, see "File Class Properties for Accessing Common Directory Locations" in Chapter 4.

The HTML component does not provide interface elements for entering or selecting URLs to load. Your application must provide other ways for the user to select the content that will be shown in the HTML component. For example, an application could present a list of URLs or web site for a user to choose from, or it could offer standard web browser interface elements such as:

- A text field for entering web page URLs
- Back and Next buttons
- A browsing history window

Here's an example that produces one of the simplest web browser applications known to man. It uses a single TextInput field for entering URLs:

```
<?xml version="1.0" encoding="utf-8"?>
<mx:ApolloApplication
     xmlns:mx="http://www.adobe.com/2006/mxml"
     layout="vertical">

     <mx:TextInput id="urlTxt" width="100%"
          enter="html.location=urlTxt.text;"
          text="http://www.adobe.com" />
     <mx:HTML id="html" width="100%" height="100%"
          location="http://www.adobe.com" />

</mx:ApolloApplication>
```

When the user enters a new URL into the text field, the enter event triggers code that sets the location property of the HTML component to the value of the text property of the TextInput field.

Loading HTML from a String

Your application can also feed HTML content to the HTML component as a string value. This allows you to use the HTML control to do advanced HTML markup and design within a Flex application. To do this, set the value of the htmlText property to a string containing valid HTML text.

The string can be a simple text string that includes some HTML tags, like this:

```
<?xml version="1.0" encoding="utf-8"?>
<mx:ApolloApplication
  xmlns:mx="http://www.adobe.com/2006/mxml"
  layout="vertical"
  creationComplete="initApp()">

  <mx:Script>
  <![CDATA[
    public function initApp():void
    {
  <application
    xmlns="http://ns.adobe.com/apollo/application/1.0.M3"
    appId="com.oreilly.apollo.examples.SampleTransparent"
    version="1.0">
      this.html.htmlText = initHtml;
    }
  ]]>
  </mx:Script>

  <mx:HTML id="html" width="100%" height="100%" />

</mx:ApolloApplication>
```

The string could also contain a full HTML page, including <html>, <head>, and <body> elements, as in this example:

```
<?xml version="1.0" encoding="utf-8"?>
<mx:ApolloApplication
  xmlns:mx="http://www.adobe.com/2006/mxml"
  layout="vertical"
  creationComplete="initApp()">

  <mx:Script>
  <![CDATA[
    public function initApp():void
    {
      var initHtml:String = "<html><head> \
           <title='Page Example'/> \
           <body bgcolor='#ccddee'><h1>Page Example</h1> \
```

```
            <p>This is a complete <b>HTML</b> \
            page as a <em>string</em>.</p></html></body>";

      this.html.htmlText = initHtml;
    }
  ]]>
  </mx:Script>

  <mx:HTML id="html" width="100%" height="100%" />

</mx:ApolloApplication>
```

The HTML markup in the string should conform to the
HTML 4 specification. The string does not need to contain
well-formed XHTML, though you can load XHTML into the
HTML component as well.

The following example shows an application that declares
XHTML content as an ActionScript XML class (using E4X
syntax), and then renders this XHTML in the HTML
component:

```
<?xml version="1.0" encoding="utf-8"?>
<mx:ApolloApplication
  xmlns:mx="http://www.adobe.com/2006/mxml"
  layout="vertical"
  creationComplete="initApp()">

  <mx:Script>
  <![CDATA[
    public function initApp():void
    {
      var initXml:XML =
        <html>
          <head>
            <title>XHTML Example</title>
          </head>
          <body bgcolor='#DDCCEE'>
            <h1>XHTML Example</h1>
            <p>This is an <b>XHTML</b> object
            converted to a <em>string</em>.</p>
          </body>
        </html>;
```

```
      this.html.htmlText = initXml.toXMLString( );
    }
  ]]>
  </mx:Script>

  <mx:HTML id="html" width="100%" height="100%" />

</mx:ApolloApplication>
```

The string that is loaded can also contain JavaScript code and CSS style declarations, or links to external JavaScript source files or stylesheets.

The HTML component fires an htmlTextChanged event whenever the htmlText property changes.

You can retrieve the HTML that was loaded as a string by getting the value of the htmlText property. The htmlText property stores the text string that was loaded.

When HTML content is loaded by setting the location property to a URL string, the htmlText property will be set to null. If you need to determine whether the current content of the HTML component was loaded from a URL or from a string, you can check the htmlText property. If it has a non-null value, then the current content was loaded from a text string; otherwise, the current content was loaded from a URL.

The application in the following example listens for the htmlTextChanged event and displays information about the source of the content that was loaded:

```
<?xml version="1.0" encoding="utf-8"?>
<mx:ApolloApplication
  xmlns:mx="http://www.adobe.com/2006/mxml"
  layout="vertical" creationComplete="initApp( )">

  <mx:Script>
    <![CDATA[
    public function initApp ( ):void
    {
      this.html.addEventListener("htmlTextChanged",
        onHtmlTextChanged);
```

```
    var initHtml:String = "<h1>htmlTextChanged Event " +
                            "Example</h1> \n" +
                            "This content started as a "+
                            "<b>HTML</b> "+
                            "<em>string</em>.";
    this.html.htmlText = initHtml;
    }

    public function onHtmlTextChanged(evt:Event):void
    {
      if (this.html.htmlText)
      {
        trace("Content was set from a string value");
      }
      else
      {
        trace("Content was loaded from a URL.");
      }
    }
    ]]>
  </mx:Script>

  <mx:TextInput id="urlTxt" width="100%"
    enter="html.location=urlTxt.text;"
    text="http://www.adobe.com" />

  <mx:HTML id="html" styleName="HTML"
    width="100%" height="100%"/>

</mx:ApolloApplication>
```

Knowing When the Location Has Changed

Your application can explicitly set the location property of the HTML component, but the location property will also change when:

- The user clicks on a hyperlink
- An HTML page automatically redirects to another page
- The window.location property of the DOM is changed by JavaScript code

When the location property changes, the HTML component dispatches a locationChange event. This event occurs before the URL location has been contacted and before any of the HTML content has been retrieved. Your application could respond to the locationChange event in order to update the display of certain UI elements before the new location is contacted, or to manipulate the URL ahead of time.

The locationChange event is the first in a series of events that occur when the location property changes. Here is the sequence of events that are triggered by setting the location property:

1. Set the location property to a URL string.
2. The locationChange event is dispatched.
3. An HTTP connection is made and data transfer begins.
4. The domInitialize event is dispatched when the initial, empty DOM is created.
5. The HTML or XHTML content is loaded.
6. External resources, such as images, are retrieved and loaded.
7. The content is rendered and an htmlRender event is dispatched. The htmlRender event can actually occur multiple times, as external resources are added to the content and the content is re-rendered.
8. The complete event is dispatched when all of the HTML content and external resources have been loaded and rendered, and after the JavaScript load event has been fired. (The load event is a standard event that is dispatched by the HTML JavaScript engine and is not something unique to Apollo.)

A similar sequence of events happen when the htmlText property is changed, though in that case the htmlTextChanged event is dispatched rather than the locationChange event.

Manipulating the HTML DOM

By listening for the domInitialize event, your application can access the initial, blank DOM before the page has loaded.

This lets it inject variables or objects into the DOM before the page elements have loaded and before any JavaScript has executed.

After the page has loaded, the HTML component will dispatch the complete event. At that point, your application can retrieve the content of the DOM using the javaScriptWindow and javaScriptDocument properties.

The javascriptWindow property represents the top-level JavaScript Window object in the DOM. The javaScriptDocument property represents the window.document object in the DOM. The window.document object contains all of the HTML content that was loaded by the HTML component.

Applying CSS Styles to the HTML Component

Like other subclasses of the UIComponent class, the HTML component can be styled using CSS style declarations. These CSS declarations affect the external appearance of the HTML component. They do not affect the HTML text or layout inside of the component. To influence the styles within an HTML document, you must use the HTML <style> tag within the content itself.

The default CSS style name for the HTML component is "HTML." The following example uses a CSS style to surround the HTML component with a 4-pixel black border:

```
<?xml version="1.0" encoding="utf 8"?>
<mx:ApolloApplication
  xmlns:mx="http://www.adobe.com/2006/mxml"
  layout="vertical">

  <mx:Style>
    .HTML {
      backgroundColor: #000000;
      paddingLeft: 4px;
      paddingRight: 4px;
      paddingTop: 4px;
      paddingBottom: 4px;
    }
  </mx:Style>
```

```
<mx:TextInput id="urlTxt" width="100%"
    enter="html.location=urlTxt.text;"
    text="http://www.adobe.com" />

<mx:HTML id="html" width="100%" height="100%"
    location="http://www.adobe.com"
    styleName="HTML" />
</mx:ApolloApplication>
```

Manipulating the HTML Component as a Sprite

The HTML component is a descendent of the DisplayObject class, so it can be placed in the display list and manipulated like any other display object. For example, your application could do any of these things to the HTML component:

- Layer it under or in between other display objects
- Apply filters to blur it, change its colors, or otherwise change its appearance
- Use matrix transformations to scale, rotate, or skew it

For an example of how to alter the display of the HTML component, see "Altering the Appearance of the HTML Component" in Chapter 5.

Accessing the Underlying HTMLControl object

There are some things that the Flex HTML component cannot do directly, such as getting or setting the scroll position, or monitoring when the content bounds change.

If your application uses a Flex HTML component, it can use the htmlControl property to reference the underlying HTMLControl object, as shown in the following example:

```
<?xml version="1.0" encoding="utf-8"?>
<mx:ApolloApplication xmlns:mx=
    "http://www.adobe.com/2006/mxml"
    layout="vertical" creationComplete="initApp()">

<mx:Script>
<![CDATA[
```

```
  public function initApp():void
  {
    html.htmlControl.addEventListener(
         HTMLEvent.CONTENT_SCROLLED,
         onHtmlScrolled);
  }

  public function onHtmlScrolled(evt:HTMLEvent):void
  {
    trace("The new scroll values are " +
         html.htmlControl.scrollX + "," +
         html.htmlControl.scrollY);
  }
]]>
</mx:Script>

<mx:TextInput id="urlTxt" width="100%"
  enter="html.location=urlTxt.text;"
  text="http://www.adobe.com" />

<mx:HTML id="html"
  width="100%" height="100%"
  location="http://www.adobe.com" />
</mx:ApolloApplication>
```

First, the initApp() method adds a listener of the
contentScroll event to the html.htmlControl object. When
the contentScroll event is received, the onHtmlScrolled()
method executes and displays the values of the underlying
HTMLControl object's scrollX and scrollY properties.

Using the HTML Control Class

It's relatively easy to drop the Flex HTML component into your
application's user interface and use it to load and browse
web pages. However, there might be times when it is easier
to work directly with the HTMLControl class in ActionScript.

This section highlights some eof the differences between the
HTMLControl class and the Flex HTML component and discusses some additional features of the HTMLControl class.

Loading HTML from a URL Location

To load HTML from a remote URL using the Flex HTML component, set the location property to a string value that contains a URL.

The HTMLControl class does things a little differently. Load content into the HTMLControl object from a remote URL by calling the load( ) method, which takes a URLRequest instance as a parameter.

The following example shows a call to the load( ) method:

```
var html:HTMLControl = new HTMLControl( );
var str:String = "http://www.oreilly.com/");
var req:URLRequest = new urlRequest(str);
html.load(req);
```

Loading a String Value Containing HTML Text

You can load a string of HTML text into an HTMLControl object by calling the loadString( ) method of the object, as in the following:

```
var simpleHtml:String =
  "<html><body><p>Hello</p></body></html>;
var html:HTMLControl = new HTMLControl( );
html.loadString(simpleHtml);
```

As with the HTML component, the string value can contain text with a few HTML tags, a complete HTML page including <html>, <head>, and <body> tags, or well-formed XHTML content.

You can also manage XHTML content using an instance of the XML class, and then use the XML.toXMLString( ) method to create a string to pass to the HTMLControl.loadString( ) method.

In most cases, the loadString( ) method, like its load( ) method counterpart, executes asynchronously, dispatching a complete event when the string has been loaded and rendered in the HTMLControl object. However, if the HTML string contains no references to outside resources, the loadString( ) method executes synchronously. That means that all of the HTML in the string is loaded and rendered in the HTMLControl object before control returns to the next line of your script. You can check whether the HTML string was loaded synchronously by using the loaded property, as shown in the following example:

```
var html:HTMLControl = new HTMLControl( );
html.loadString(content);
if (html.loaded)
{
  trace( "The loadString( ) method was synchronous." );
}
```

Even if the loadString( ) method executes synchronously, it causes a complete event to be dispatched when the content is loaded and rendered.

Manipulating the HTML DOM

As with the HTML component, the HTMLControl class dispatches a domInitialize event when the initial, blank DOM object is created, and it dispatches a complete event when the HTML page is fully loaded and rendered.

After either of these events, your application can access the DOM from the HTMLControl object by using the window property, which represents the top-level JavaScript Window object.

After the complete event has been received, the DOM will be fully populated. The window.document property will contain all of the HTML content that was loaded by the HTML component.

Knowing When the Content Bounds Change

The content bounds represent the size of the rendered HTML content, not including scroll bars. These bounds can change when new content is loaded into an existing page. For example, a script could load a new image into a space that is currently smaller than the new image. In that case, the positions of other HTML elements might shift to accommodate the larger image, thereby enlarging the overall content bounds.

Your application can recognize a bounds change by listening for the `htmlBoundsChange` event from the `HTMLControl` class.

Script Bridging: Communicating Between ActionScript and JavaScript

One exciting feature of Apollo is the ability to easily cross-script between ActionScript code (in SWF files) and JavaScript code (in HTML).

ActionScript code in a SWF file can access the HTML DOM (document object model) and the JavaScript code in an HTML page loaded as a child object of the SWF file. Similarly, JavaScript code in an HTML page loaded into an `HTMLControl` object (or a Flex HTML component) can access ActionScript content from the parent SWF file.

In addition, HTML content loaded in Apollo can access the built-in ActionScript classes.

There are a number of potential uses for this:

- ActionScript code can inspect and alter the DOM of an HTML page.
- ActionScript code can get or set JavaScript variables in an HTML page. They can also call JavaScript methods.
- An HTML page can access ActionScript objects and methods in the SWF file that contains it.
- JavaScript in an HTML page can call any built-in class in ActionScript 3.0. For example, it could instantiate a new Sound or Socket object.

Manipulating the DOM from ActionScript

When the HTML content is loaded, it dispatches the complete event. At that point, you can examine and manipulate the DOM.

For example, consider the following simple HTML document:

```
<html>
  <style>
    .test { fontFamily:"Arial"; fontSize:"12" }
  </style>
  <body>
    <p id="p1">Hi,
          <span id="userName" class="test">
              Bob</span>.
      </p>
  </body>
</html>
```

After the HTMLControl object that loads this HTML dispatches the complete event, your application can manipulate the DOM, as shown here:

```
var html:HTMLControl = new HTMLControl();
var urlReq:URLRequest = new URLRequest("test.html");
html.load(urlReq);
html.addEventListener(Event.COMPLETE, completeHandler);

private function completeHandler(event:Event):void {
  var doc:JavaScriptObject = html.window.document;
  doc.getElementById("userName").innerHTML = "Sue";
}
```

The html.window.document property is returned as an instance of the JavaScriptObject class. A JavaScriptObject references a specific object in the HTML page, and it lets your ActionScript code call any method or access any property of that object.

In most cases, it is simplest to use ActionScript dot notation to directly reference properties and methods of the DOM.

The following example shows how to access details of a style declaration:

```
html.window.document.styleSheets[0].cssRules[0].style.
fontSize = "32";
```

Listening for JavaScript Events from ActionScript

You can register an ActionScript function as a JavaScript event handler, which lets you call ActionScript methods directly from JavaScript code.

For example, consider this simple HTML page:

```
<html>
  <body>
    <a id="myLink" href="http://www.oreilly.com">Test</a>
  </body>
</html>
```

In the following sample application, the HTMLControl object loads this HTML content and then dispatches the complete event, triggering the completeHandler( ) method. The completeHandler( ) method gets a reference to the myLink JavaScript object, which represents a hyperlink anchor tag in the DOM. It then sets the anchor tag's onclick handle to point to the clickHandler( ) method in the ActionScript code (which will, by the way, erase the existing onclick event handler, if there was one). As a result, when the user clicks on the hyperlink, the clickHandler( ) method is called:

```
var html:HTMLControl = new HTMLControl( );
var xhtml:XML =
  <html>
    <body>
      <a id="myLink" href="#">Test</a>
    </body>
  </html>;

html.addEventListener(Event.COMPLETE, completeHandler);

html.loadString(xhtml.toXMLString( ));
```

```
private function completeHandler(event:Event):void {
  var myLink:Object = html.window.document.
getElementById("myLink");
  myLink.onclick = clickHandler;
}

private function clickHandler(event:Object):void {
  trace("clicked");
}
```

TIP

You can also use DOM Level 2 event handling, although
that support was not finalized for the Alpha 1 release at
the time this book was written.

Calling JavaScript Functions from ActionScript

Once an HTML component (or an HTMLControl object) dispatches the complete event, you can call its functions from
ActionScript.

For example, the following code calls the JavaScript alert( )
method when the HTML page is loaded:

```
var html:HTMLControl = new HTMLControl( );
var urlReq:URLRequest = new URLRequest("test.html");
html.addEventListener(EventComplete, completeHandler);

private function completeHandler (event: Event):void {
    html.window.alert("Hello from ActionScript.");
}
```

You can also call custom JavaScript functions and access
JavaScript properties in an HTML page. For example, consider the following HTML document:

```
<html>
  <script>
    greeting = "hello";
    function reverseStr(str) {
      returnStr = "";
      for (i = 0; i < str.length; i++) {
        returnStr = str.charAt(i) + returnStr;
```

```
    }
    return returnStr;
  }
</script>
<body>
  <p>Test page</p>
</body>
</html>
```

From ActionScript, you can access the JavaScript variable named greeting and the JavaScript reverseStr( ) function after the HTMLControl object dispatches a complete event:

```
var html:HTMLControl = new HTMLControl( );
var urlReq:URLRequest = new URLRequest("test.html");
htmlControlObj.addEventListener(Event.COMPLETE,
completeHandler);

private function completeHandler(event:Event):void {
    trace(html.window.greeting); // hello
    trace(html.window.reverseStr("foo")); // oof
}
```

Calling ActionScript Functions from JavaScript

A powerful feature in the Apollo runtime is the ability to call ActionScript from JavaScript. JavaScript in the HTML page loaded by an HTMLControl object can call the methods and properties of the parent ActionScript object that contains the HTMLControl object. It can also call built-in ActionScript classes and methods. This is done using a JavaScript object named runtime, which is available to any JavaScript content loaded in the Apollo runtime.

For example, the following JavaScript code calls the Action-Script trace( ) method:

```
runtime.trace("Hello from JavaScript.");
```

This script-bridging feature exposes a wealth of useful ActionScript features to JavaScript code. For example, the following JavaScript example uses the ActionScript Sound class to play an MP3 file:

```
urlReq = new runtime.flash.net.URLRequest("test.mp3");
sound = new runtime.flash.media.Sound(urlReq);
sound.play();
```

To allow this kind of JavaScript-to-ActionScript script bridging, you must set the exposeRuntime property of the HTMLControl object to true:

```
var html:HTMLControl = new HTMLControl();
html.attachexposeRuntime = true;
```

TIP

The Apollo SDK will include JavaScript classes that make calling Apollo and ActionScript APIs a little more intuitive. This is not included in Apollo Alpha 1.

CHAPTER 4

Using the File System API

Apollo provides a file I/O API that lets applications read and write files and directories on the user's computer. The file I/O API includes the following functionality:

- Create and delete files and directories
- Copy and move files and directories
- List the contents of directories
- Get system information on files and directories
- Read and write binary files
- Read and write text files
- Serialize and deserialize ActionScript objects

The low-level functionality for working with the file system is accessed via ActionScript. The Flex framework for Apollo includes components for working with files and directories, but these are graphical components for navigating the file system and selecting files and directories. They do not provide direct access to the more fundamental file I/O operations.

In addition to the information in this chapter, see the examples presented in "Working with the File System" in Chapter 5. Those examples illustrate many of the concepts described in this chapter, and they provide working MXML code that you can test, using Flex Builder or the Apollo SDK.

Security Model

Apollo will eventually provide a complete security model for managing access to local resources, such as the file system. However, this security model has not been implemented in the Apollo Alpha 1 build.

It is important to remember that Apollo applications are installed to and run from the user's computer. Apollo applications have a different security context and security model than those of web browsers. Because of this, the same rules that apply to downloading and running other applications also apply to downloading and running Apollo applications. Users should download and install applications only from trusted sources.

Accessing Files and Directories

Apollo applications can run on multiple platforms, including Windows and Mac OS. The Apollo file API uses platform-neutral code syntax so you don't have to write any OS-specific code.

For example, the way you represent a path to a file differs between Mac OS and Windows:

- A typical file path on Mac OS is */Users/joe/Documents/test.txt*

- A typical file path on Windows is *C:\Documents and Settings\joe\My Documents\test.txt*

However, you can use exactly the same Apollo components, classes, methods, and properties to access files in either operating system.

An ActionScript File object is a pointer to a file or directory. The File class includes the static property documentsDirectory, which contains a File object that points to the user's documents directory. This is the *My Documents* directory on Windows, and it is the *Documents* subdirectory of the user directory on Mac OS, as illustrated in the following code:

```
trace(File.documentsDirectory.nativePath)
    // On Windows:
    //      C:\Documents and Settings\joe\MyDocuments
    // On Mac OS:  /Users/joe/Documents
```

Once you point a File object to a directory, you can use the resolve() method to modify it to point to a file or subdirectory within that directory (or within a subdirectory). For example, the following code creates an *Apollo Test* subdirectory of the user's documents directory:

```
var newDir:File = File.documentsDirectory;
newDir = newDir.resolve("ApolloTest");
newDir.createDirectory();
```

A File object can point to either a file or a directory. Also, a File object may point to a file or directory that does not exist, as in the previous example. This lets you point a File object to a directory location that you wish to create.

File Class Properties for Accessing Common Directory Locations

The File class includes the following static properties, which point to commonly used directory locations:

Property	Description
File.appStorageDirectory	Each installed Apollo application is given a unique *application storage directory*. This is a good place to store files that the application may want to maintain but that the user will probably need not see. This may include log files, cache files, and preferences files.
File.appResourceDirectory	The application's install directory.
File.currentDirectory	This is the directory from which the file was launched. You may use this property to resolve the file path of any command-line parameters that were passed to the application.
File.desktopDirectory	This is the user's desktop directory.

Property	Description
File.documentsDirectory	This is the *My Documents* directory on Windows, and the *Documents* subdirectory of the user directory on Mac OS.
File.userDirectory	This is the user's home directory. For example, on Mac OS, it is the *Users/ username* directory, and on Windows it is typically *c:\\Document and Settings\ username*.

The url and nativePath Properties of a File Object

The url property of a File object returns the location of a file or folder as a platform-independent string that begins with a URL scheme, such as file, as in the following:

```
var directory:File = File.userDirectory;
trace(directory.url)
   // on Windows: file:///C:/Documents%20and%20Settings
   // on Mac OS: file:///Users
```

whereas the nativePath property of a File object returns a string that is unique to Windows or Mac OS. For example, you can use this code to point to a specific file on a Windows computer:

```
var file:File = new File( );
file.nativePath = "c:/ApolloTest/surprise.txt";
```

However, it is generally better to start with one of the static properties listed in the table in the previous section (such as the File.appStorageDirectory)—that point to known directories on the operating system—and then use the resolve( ) method to create to a relative path based on that directory, as in this code:

```
var logFile:File = File.appStorageDirectory;
logFile = logFile.resolve("log.txt");
```

Use the application store directory to store files that you want your application to be able to access in the future but that the end user may not need to know about. For instance, this is a good place to store preferences files.

URI Schemes

A URI scheme is specified at the beginning of a URL, such as
file in the following example:

```
file:///c:/ApolloTest/test.txt
```

In addition to the file URI scheme, Apollo supports the new
URI schemes app-storage and app-resource.

app-storage

Identifies the application storage directory, as shown in the
following example:

```
var logFile:File = File.appStorageDirectory;
logFile = logFile.resolve("log.txt");
trace(logFile.url); // app-storage:/log.txt
```

app-resource

Identifies this application's installation folder, as in the
following:

```
var installDir:File = new File();
installDir.url = "app-resource:/";
installDir = installDir.resolve("HelloWorld-app.xml");
trace(installDir.url); // app-resource:/HelloWorld-app.xml
```

file

The url property of other File object returns a standard file
URL scheme:

```
var file:File = File.documentsDirectory;
file = file.resolve("ApolloTest/test.txt");
trace(file.url);
  // On Windows:
  // file:///C:/Documents%20and %20Settings/ ... /test.txt
  // On Mac OS:
  // file:///Users/userName/Documents/ ... /test.txt
```

Asynchronous and Synchronous Versions of Methods

Some of the methods of the File class (such as File. copyFile( ) and File.copyFileAsync( )) and of the FileStream class have both synchronous and asynchronous versions.

The synchronous methods don't relinquish control until the file operation is complete. The asynchronous methods run in the background, allowing other ActionScript processes to take place at the same time. When the asynchronous file operation finishes, an event is dispatched to notify listeners that it is done.

Here's an example of copying a file using the synchronous copyTo( ) method:

```
var file1:File = File.documentsDirectory.
resolve("ApolloTest/test.txt");
var file2:File = File.documentsDirectory.
resolve("ApolloTest/copy of test.txt");
file1.copyTo(file2);
trace("Not output until the file is copied.");
```

Here's an example of copying a file using the asynchronous copyToAsync( ) method:

```
var file1:File = File.documentsDirectory.
resolve("ApolloTest/test.txt");
var file2:File = File.documentsDirectory.
resolve("ApolloTest/copy of test.txt");
file1.copyToAsync(file2);

file1.addEventListener(Event.COMPLETE, completeHandler);
trace("This line executes before the complete event.");
trace("So does this line.");

private function completeHandler(event:Event):void {
  trace("Done.");
}
```

The following table lists the asynchronous methods of the File class (all of which have synchronous counterparts) and the events that can fire after the method is called:

Asynchronous File method	Events
copyToAsync( )	complete, ioError
deleteDirectoryAsync( )	complete, ioError
deleteFileAsync( )	complete, ioError
listDirectoryAsync( )	directoryListing, ioError
moveToAsync( )	complete, ioError
moveToTrashAsync( )	complete, ioError

When you open a file, use either the open( ) or openAsync( ) method of the FileStream object. The first opens the file for synchronous operations, and the second opens the file for asynchronous operations. For more information, see "The open( ) and openAsync( ) Methods" later in this chapter.

Use asynchronous methods whenever you want to make sure that other essential ActionScript-driven processes—such as progress bar animation—continue while the file operations take place. For example, you could use the open( ) (synchronous) method of a FileStream object if you are going to write a small file (1 MB or less) and use the openAsync( ) method when writing larger files, or when the file size is unknown.

For more information on asynchronous methods in general, see the "Handling Events" chapter in *Programming ActionScript 3.0*, which is available at:

http://livedocs.macromedia.com/flex/2/docs/Part5_ProgAS.html

Reading Directory Contents

The File.listDirectory( ) method returns an array listing of File objects that represent the files and directories contained within the specified directory. For example, the following code lists the contents of the desktop directory:

```
var directory:File = File.desktopDirectory;
var contents:Array = directory.listDirectory();
for (var i:uint = 0; i < contents.length; i++) {
    if (contents[i].isDirectory) {
        trace(contents[i].name);
    } else {
        trace(contents[i].name,
        contents[i].size,
        "bytes");
    }
}
```

The File.listDirectory() method returns only the root level files and directories in a directory. It does not recursively search through subdirectories for their contents. You can, of course, write code to traverse subdirectories, though if you do so, you might want to use the File.listDirectoryAsync() method so that other ActionScript-driven processes can continue while the directory listings are being compiled.

Also see "Getting a Directory Listing" in Chapter 5.

Getting File Information

The File class includes a number of properties that contain information about a file or directory.

Property	Description
exists	States whether the file or directory exists. This is worth checking, for example, before you attempt to read, write, copy, or move a file.
isDirectory	States whether the File object points to a directory (true) or a file (false). You will want to check this before attempting directory-specific operations (such as the listDirectory() method) or attempting file-specific operations (such as reading a file).
isHidden	States whether the file or directory is hidden.
nativePath	Notes the operating system-specific path to the file or directory.
parent	Notes the parent directory of the File instance.
url	Notes the operating system-independent path to the file or directory.

The File class also inherits the following useful properties from the FileReference class:

Property	Description
creationDate	The date the file or folder was created.
modificationDate	The date when the file was last modified.
name	The file or folder name.
size	The size of the file, in bytes.

Copying and Moving Files and Directories

The File.copyTo( ) and File.moveTo( ) methods copy or move a file or directory to a specified new location. For example, the following code copies the *test.txt* file in the *Apollo Test* subdirectory of the user's documents directory to the *User Data* subdirectory of the application storage directory:

```
var file1:File = File.documentsDirectory.resolve("Apollo
Test/test.txt");
var destination:File = File.appStorageDirectory.
resolve("User Data");
destination.createDirectory( );
var file2:File = destination.resolve("test.txt");
file1.copyTo(file2);
```

Note the call to the File.createDirectory( ) method, which ensures that the destination directory exists.

The following code moves the *Apollo Test 1* subdirectory of the user's documents directory to the *Apollo Test 2* subdirectory (effectively renaming the directory):

```
var dir1:File = File.documentsDirectory;
dir1 = dir1.resolve("Apollo Test 1");
var dir2:File = File.documentsDirectory;
dir2 = dir2.resolve("Apollo Test 2");
```

You might want to use the asynchronous versions of these methods, `File.copyToAsync()` and `File.moveToAsync()`, if the copy or move operation could take a long time.

Each of these methods includes a `clobber` parameter, which you can set to `true` to have the operation overwrite existing files. By default, this parameter is set to `false`.

Creating Files and Directories

The `File.createTempFile()` and `File.createTempDirectory()` static methods of the `File` class let you create a temporary file or directory. Apollo ensures that the temporary file or directory created by these methods is new and unique. For example, the following code creates a temporary file:

```
var bufferStorage:File = File.createTempFile();
```

Temporary files and directories are not automatically deleted when you close an Apollo application. You will generally want to delete temporary files and directories before closing the application. See the next section, "Deleting Files and Directories," for more details.

The `File.createDirectory()` method lets you create a directory in the location specified by the `File` object:

```
var directory = File.documentsDirectory;
directory = directory.resolve("ApolloTest");
```

When you open a `FileStream` object with write capabilities then directories are created automatically, if needed. For more information about `FileStream` objects, see "Reading and Writing Files" later in this chapter.

Deleting Files and Directories

The `File.deleteFile()` method permanently deletes a file, and the `File.deleteDirectory()` method permanently deletes a directory. The `File.moveToTrash()` method lets you move a file or directory to the system trash.

Each of these methods also has an asynchronous counterpart.

Reading and Writing Files

The `FileStream` class provides methods that let your application read and write files.

Here's the general process for reading and writing to a file:

1. Set up a `File` object that points to the file you want to read or write.

   For details, see "Accessing Files and Directories," earlier in this chapter.

2. Instantiate a `FileStream` object—for example:

   ```
   var stream:FileStream = new FileStream();.
   ```

3. Call the `FileStream.open()` or `FileStream.openAsync()` method, passing in the `File` object as the `file` parameter and passing an appropriate file mode as the `fileMode` parameter. For example:

   ```
   stream.open(file, FileMode.READ);
   ```

   For more information, see "File Open Modes" later in this chapter.

4. If you called the `FileStream.openAsync()` method, set up the appropriate event listener functions.

   For more information, see "The open() and openAsync() Methods," next.

5. Call the appropriate read and write method for your data.

   For more information, see "Read and Write Methods" later in this chapter

6. Close the file, using the `FileStream.close()` method. For example:

   ```
   stream.close();
   ```

Steps 3, 4, and 5 are described in more detail the sections that follow. First, here is a sample of code for reading UTF-8 text from a file synchronously:

```
var file:File = File.appStorageDirectory;
file = file.resolve("settings.xml");
var stream:FileStream = new FileStream();
stream.open(file, FileMode.READ);
var data:String = stream.readUTFBytes(stream.
bytesAvailable);
stream.close();
```

Here is some code that reads the same data asynchronously:

```
var file:File = File.appStorageDirectory;
file = file.resolve("settings.xml");
var stream:FileStream = new FileStream();
stream.openAsync(file, FileMode.READ);
stream.addEventListener(Event.COMPLETE, readData);
var data:String;

private function readData(event:Event):void {
  data = stream.readUTFBytes(stream.bytesAvailable);
  stream.close();
}
```

The open( ) and openAsync( ) Methods

Your application needs to open a file before it can read from or write to the file.

When you open a file with the FileStream.openAsync( ) method, the file is opened for asynchronous operations, and you've registered event listeners to monitor progress.

The FileStream.open( ) method opens the file for synchronous operations. If your application opens the file using this synchronous method, all subsequent calls to methods that read or write to the file will be done synchronously as well. In the following example, each of the calls to stream.open( ), stream.writeUTFBytes( ), and stream.close( ) will complete before the next call is made.

```
var newFile:File = File.documentsDirectory;
file = file.resolve("ApolloTest/test.txt");
```

```
var stream:FileStream = new FileStream()
stream.open(file, FileMode.WRITE);
stream.writeUTFBytes("This is some sample text.");
stream.close();
```

The advantage of opening a file for synchronous operations is that you can write less code to complete a task. The disadvantage is that execution of other ActionScript code can be delayed if the file operations take a while. As a result, if you are working with large files or opening files that are shared on slow networks, you should consider using the FileStream.openAsync() method instead.

When you use the openAsync() method, the following processes are all handled asynchronously:

Closing the file
> The FileStream object dispatches a close event when the file is closed.

Reading data into the read buffer
> The FileStream object dispatches progress events as data is read, and it dispatches a complete event once all the data is read. However, once data is read, calling a read method (such as readBytes()) to read data is a synchronous process.

I/O errors
> The FileStream object dispatches an ioError event upon encountering an error. This may occur for a number of reasons, such as attempting to open a file that doesn't exist or attempting to write to a file that is locked. However, some errors, such as attempting to read from a file that has not been opened, throw exceptions (rather than dispatch ioError events) because the Apollo runtime can detect the error condition instantly.

Before calling the FileStream.openAsync() method, your application should set up event listener functions to handle those events in which it is interested.

The following example opens a file in asynchronous read mode. After the file has been opened, the complete event will be dispatched (unless there is an error, in which case the ioError event will be dispatched instead). The completeHandler() method then calls the FileStream. readBytes() method, which starts reading data from the file as an array of bytes, in asynchronous mode. When all the bytes have been read from the file, the complete event will be dispatched:

```
var file:File = File.documentsDirectory.
resolve("ApolloTest/test.txt");
var stream:FileStream = new FileStream();

stream.addEventListener(ProgressEvent.PROGRESS,
progressHandler);
stream.addEventListener(Event.COMPLETE, completeHandler);
stream.addEventListener(IOErrorEvent.IO_ERROR, ioErrorHandler);
stream.addEventListener(Event.CLOSE, closeHandler);

stream.openAsync(file, FileMode.READ);

var data:ByteArray = new ByteArray();

private function progressHandler(event:ProgressEvent):void {
    trace(stream.bytesAvailable, "bytes read.");
}
private function completeHandler(event: Event):void {
    data = stream.readBytes(stream.bytesAvailable);
    stream.close();
}
private function ioErrorHandler(event:IOErrorEvent):void {
    trace("An I/O error was encountered.");
}
private function closeHandler(event: Event):void {
    trace("File closed.");
}
```

File Open Modes

The FileStream.open() method and FileStream.openAsync() method both accept two parameters: the file parameter corresponding to the file that you want to open, and the fileMode parameter, which is a string defining the capabilities of the FileStream object. The possible values for the fileMode parameter are defined as constants in the FileMode class.

For example, the following code opens the file synchronously for write operations, but not for read operations:

```
stream.open(file, FileMode.WRITE);
```

Here are the FileMode constants and their meanings:

FileMode constant	Definition
FileMode.APPEND	The file is opened in write-only mode, with all written data appended to the end of the file. Upon opening, any non-existent file is created.
FileMode.READ	The file is opened in read-only mode. The file must exist (missing files are not created).
FileMode.UPDATE	The file is opened in read/write mode, and data can be written to any position in the file or appended to the end. Upon opening, any nonexistent file is created.
FileMode.WRITE	The file is opened in write-only mode. If the file does not exist, it will be created. If the file does exist, it will be overwritten.

Read and Write Methods

The FileStream class includes a number of read and write methods, each corresponding to the format of the data being read or written. For example, you can use the readUTFBytes() and writeUTFBytes() methods to read or write an array of bytes, whereas the readByte() and writeByte() methods read or write a single byte at a time. All in all, there are 26 read and write methods. For details on each, see the description of these methods in the *ActionScript 3.0 Language Reference*, which is distributed with Apollo Alpha 1.

Even though reading and writing text data may seem trivial, you should consider the encoding of the text in the file. The readUTFBytes() and writeUTFBytes() methods provide means to read and write UTF-8–encoded text. The `readMultiByte()` and `writeMultiByte()` methods let you specify a different character encoding for the file data. There are other factors to consider as well. For example, a UTF file may start with a UTF byte order mark (BOM) character, which defines the UTF encoding and the byte order (or "endianness") of the data.

For more information, see the "Data formats, and choosing the read and write methods to use" section of the *Apollo Developer's Guide* (*http://www.adobe.com/go/apollodocs*).

More Information

For examples of reading and writing files, see the following sections in Chapter 5:

- "Writing a Text File from a String"
- "Reading a Text File into a String"
- "Encoding Bitmap Data into PNG or JPEG Format and Writing It to the File System"
- "Serializing and De-Serializing ActionScript Objects to the File System"

Apollo Mini-Cookbook

This chapter describes solutions to common tasks in Apollo applications. The solutions in this chapter illustrate many concepts described in previous chapters, and it provides working MXML code that you can test using Flex Builder or the Apollo SDK.

Working with the File System

Apollo lets you access the file system on the user's computer. This section of the cookbook shows some solutions to common tasks when working with the file system.

For a conceptual overview of the Apollo file system capabilities, see "Accessing the File System."

Writing a Text File from a String

Problem

You want to synchronously write data from an ActionScript String object to a text file.

Solution

Call an appropriate write method, such as writeUTF( ), of a FileStream object.

Discussion

This example uses a File object named file, which represents a *test.txt* file in the Apollo Test subdirectory of the user's documents directory:

```
var file:File = File.documentsDirectory
file = file.resolve("Apollo Test/test.txt");
```

For more information, see "Accessing the File System."

The FileStream class is used to open, read, write, and close files. You pass a fileMode parameter to the open( ) method (or to the openAsync( ) method, if you want the operation to occur asyncronously) to specify the capabilities of the FileStream object. In this case, FileMode.WRITE provides write access to the file:

```
var stream:FileStream = new FileStream( )
stream.open(file, FileMode.WRITE);
```

TIP

The FileMode.APPEND and FileMode.UPDATE modes also provide write access. This example uses the FileMode. WRITE mode because it creates the file if it does not exist and overwrites any existing data. For more information, see the description of the FileMode class in the *Action-Script 3.0 Language Reference* provided with the Apollo documentation.

There are a number of read and write methods in the FileStream class. This example uses the writeUTFBytes( ) method, which writes a string to a file using UTF-8 character encoding.

You could also use the writeMultiByte( ) method, which lets you specify a character encoding to use for the data. For example, the following code writes data using the default encoding used by the host operating system:

```
stream.writeMultiByte(file, File.systemCharset);
```

Here the `File.systemCharset` property is passed as the `charSet` parameter of the `readMultiByte()` method. Apollo supports other character encodings, such as "shift-jis" and "iso-8859-1." For more information, see the "Supported Character Sets" appendix in the *ActionScript 3.0 Language Reference* provided with the Apollo documentation.

Note that the code replaces return (\r) and linefeed (\n) characters in the string with the appropriate line-ending character for the system (which is available via the `File.lineEnding` static property):

```
str = str.replace(/[\r|\n]/g, File.lineEnding);
```

For the line-ending text files in Windows, use the carriage return character (\r), followed by the line-feed character (\n). In Mac OS, only the line feed (\n) character is used.

Here is the full MXML code for a simple application that writes a UTF-8-encoded text file from a string:

```
<?xml version="1.0" encoding="utf-8"?>
<mx:ApolloApplication xmlns:mx="http://www.adobe.com/2006/
mxml" layout="vertical">
    <mx:Script>
        <![CDATA[
            import flash.filesystem.*;
            public function saveData():void {
                var file:File = File.documentsDirectory;
                file = file.resolve("Apollo Test/test.txt");
                var stream:FileStream = new FileStream( )
                stream.open(file, FileMode.WRITE);

                var str:String = input.text;
                str = str.replace(/\r/g, File.lineEnding);

                stream.writeUTFBytes(str);
                stream.close();
                trace("File written.");

            }
        ]]>
    </mx:Script>
```

```
    <mx:TextArea id="input" width="100%" height="100%"
      text="Type text here."/>
    <mx:Button label="Save" click="saveData()" />
</mx:ApolloApplication>
```

Reading a Text File into a String

Problem

You want to synchronously read data from a text file into an
ActionScript String object.

Solution

Call an appropriate read method, such as readUTF(), of a
FileStream object.

Discussion

This example uses a File object named file, which points to
the *test.txt* file in the Apollo Test subdirectory of the user's
documents directory:

```
var file:File = File.documentsDirectory
file = file.resolve("Apollo Test/test.txt");
```

The FileStream class is used to open, read, write, and close
files. Pass a fileMode parameter to the open() method (or
openAsync() method if you want the read to happen asyncronously) to specify the capabilities of the FileStream object.
In this case, FileMode.READ provides read access to the file:

```
stream = new FileStream();
stream.open(file, FileMode.READ);
```

TIP

The FileMode.UPDATE mode also provides read access to
the file. However, it also provides write access, which we
do not want for this example, so the example uses the
FileMode.READ mode. For more information, see the
description of the FileMode class in the *ActionScript 3.0
Language Reference* provided with the Apollo
documentation.

There are a number of read and write methods in the FileStream class. This code uses the readUTFBytes( ) method, which reads a string to from the read buffer UTF-8 character encoding.

You could also use the readMultiByte( ) method, which lets you specify a character encoding to use for interpreting the data. For example, the following code reads data using the default encoding used by the host operating system:

```
Str = stream.readMultiByte(file, File.systemCharset);
```

Here the File.systemCharset property is passed as the charSet parameter of the readMultiByte( ) method. Apollo supports other character encodings, such as "shift-jis" and "iso-8859-1". Your choice of character encoding depends on the format of the data in the file. For more information, see the "Supported Character Sets" appendix in the *ActionScript 3.0 Language Reference* provided with the Apollo documentation.

Note that the code replaces the operating system-specific line ending character (which is available via the File.lineEnding static property) with the line-feed character (\n), which you use in text fields in SWF files:

```
str = str.replace(File.lineEnding, "\n");
```

For the line-ending text files in Windows, use the carriage return character (\r), followed by the line-feed character (\n). In Mac OS, only the line feed character is used.

Here is the complete MXML code for an application that reads a UTF-8-encoded text file into a string:

```
<?xml version="1.0" encoding="utf-8"?>
<mx:ApolloApplication xmlns:mx="http://www.adobe.com/2006/
mxml" layout="vertical">
    <mx:Script>
        <![CDATA[
            import flash.filesystem.*;
            public var stream:FileStream;
            public function readFile():void {
                var file:File = File.documentsDirectory;
```

```
            file = file.resolve("Apollo Test/test.txt");
            stream = new FileStream();
            stream.open(file, FileMode.READ);
            var str:String = stream.
              readUTFBytes(stream.bytesAvailable);
            stream.close();
            str = str.replace(File.lineEnding, "\n");
            log.text = str;
        }

    ]]>
  </mx:Script>
  <mx:TextArea id="log" width="100%" height="100%"/>
  <mx:Button label="Open" click="readFile()" />
</mx:ApolloApplication>
```

Encoding Bitmap Data into PNG or JPEG Format and Writing It to the File System

Problem

You want to save bitmap data from an Apollo application to a *.png* or *.jpg* file, which can be opened by other applications.

Solution

Download the JPEGEncoder class or PNGEncoder class from the open source corelib library, and then pass an ActionScript BitmapData object to the encode() method of the JPEGEncoder or PNGEncoder class. Then pass the ByteArray object returned by the encode() method to the writeBytes() method of a FileStream object.

Discussion

One of the benefits of ActionScript is the ability to write reusable class libraries. At the Adobe Labs web site, the corelib project includes classes for MD5 hashing, JSON serialization, advanced string and date parsing, and more.

Included in the corelib project are classes for JPEG and PNG encoding.

Although Apollo files can load and display graphics, there are no built-in routines for converting bitmap images to JPEG or PNG format. The JPEGEncoder and PNGEncoder classes, posted on the Adobe Labs web site, provide this functionality.

1. Download the *corelib.zip* file from the project site at Google Code:

    http://code.google.com/p/as3corelib/

2. Unzip the file.

3. Copy the *src/com* directory from the ZIP file to your project directory, so that a *com* directory is created within the project directory.

This file loads a JPG file named *test.jpg* into a Flex Image component:

```
<mx:Image id="img" source="test.jpg" />
```

The user clicks the Blur button, which applies a blur filter to the Image object (by adding a new BlurFilter object to the filters array of the Image object):

```
var filter:BlurFilter = new BlurFilter();
img.filters = [filter];
```

When the user clicks the Save button, the application begins processing the graphic. First, the data from the image is converted to a BitmapData object, which is then passed to the encode() method of a JPEGEncoder object:

```
var bmpData:BitmapData =
  new BitmapData(img.width, img.height);
bmpData.draw(img);
var jpgEncoder:JPEGEncoder = new JPEGEncoder();
var jpgBytes:ByteArray = jpgEncoder.encode(bmpData);
```

Next, the byte array returned by the call to the encode() method is written to a file:

```
var file:File = File.desktopDirectory.resolve("test-blur.jpg");
vr stream:FileStream = new FileStream();
stream.open(file, FileMode.WRITE);
stream.writeBytes(jpgBytes, 0, jpgBytes.length);
stream.close();
```

The code File.desktopDirectory.resolve("test-blur.jpg") returns a File object pointing to the *blurred.jpg* file on the user's desktop. The FileStream object is opened to that file in write mode, and the writeBytes() method writes the byte array data to the file.

Here is the full MXML code for the example. Note that you will need link in the JPEGEncoder class, as specified earlier:

```
<?xml version="1.0" encoding="utf-8"?>
<mx:ApolloApplication xmlns:mx="http://www.adobe.com/2006/
  mxml" layout="vertical">
    <mx:Script>
        <![CDATA[
            import flash.filesystem.*;
            import com.adobe.images.JPEGEncoder;
            public function blurImage():void {
                var filter:BlurFilter = new BlurFilter();
                img.filters = [filter];

            }
            public function saveImg():void {
                var bmpData:BitmapData = new
                    BitmapData(img.width, img.height);
                bmpData.draw(img);
                var jpgEncoder:JPEGEncoder = new
                  JPEGEncoder();
                var jpgBytes:ByteArray =
                  jpgEncoder.encode(bmpData);
                var file:File =
                  File.desktopDirectory.resolve("blurred.jpg");
                var stream:FileStream = new FileStream();
                stream.open(file, FileMode.WRITE);
                stream.writeBytes(jpgBytes, 0,
                  jpgBytes.length);
                stream.close();
            }
        ]]>
    </mx:Script>
    <mx:Image id="img" source="test.jpg" />
    <mx:Button label="Blur" click="blurImage()" />
    <mx:Button label="Save" click="saveImg()" />
</mx:ApolloApplication>
```

Serializing and De-Serializing ActionScript Objects to the File System

Problem

You want to save data from an ActionScript object in an Apollo application to a file, and subsequently open that file to reconstruct the ActionScript object.

Solution

Use the `writeObject()` and `readObject()` methods of the `FileStream` class.

Discussion

The `writeObject()` and `readObject()` methods of the `FileStream` class let you serialize and de-serialize any Action-Script object to a file. The object is serialized to the file system in the Action Message Format (AMF).

Here is the code for a simple example that serializes and de-serializes a `Dictionary` instance to the file system.

First, we register the `Dictionary` type with the player:

```
registerClassAlias("flash.utils.Dictionary", Dictionary);
```

The `registerClassAlias` API ensures that the class type of the object instance is encoded and saved with serialized data. If the class type is not registered, the serialized class instance is treated as an object type.

Next we create a file instance that points to the file where the serialized object will be stored (in this case, a file named *data.db* in the application storage directory):

```
data_file = File.appStorageDirectory.resolve("data.db");
```

When the serialize button is pressed, the code creates and populates a `Dictionary` object, and then uses the `writeObject` method of the FileStream class to write the object out to the file system in AMF format:

```
private function onSerializeClick(event:MouseEvent):void
{
    var d:Dictionary = new Dictionary();
        d["key_a"] = "value_a";
        d["key_b"] = "value_b";
        d["key_c"] = "value_c";
        d["key_d"] = "value_d";

    var fs:FileStream = new FileStream();
        fs.open(data_file, FileMode.WRITE);
        fs.writeObject(d);
        fs.close();

}
```

When the Deserialize button is pressed, the serialized Dictionary is read from the file system and prints out its values:

```
var d:Dictionary;

if(!data_file.exists)
{
    outfield.text += "Serialized Data File
    does not exist : " +
    data_file.nativePath + "\n";
}

var fs:FileStream = new FileStream();
    fs.open(data_file, FileMode.READ);
    d = (fs.readObject() as Dictionary);
    fs.close();

  outfield.text += "Dictionary de-serialized\n";

    for (var key:String in d)
    {
    outfield.text += key + " : " + d[key] + "\n";
    }
```

Note that we first check and make sure that the serialized file exists. Here is the complete code:

```
<?xml version="1.0" encoding="utf-8"?>
<mx:ApolloApplication xmlns:mx="http://www.adobe.com/2006/
mxml" layout="absolute"
        creationComplete="onCreationComplete( )">

    <mx:Script>
        <![CDATA[
            import flash.filesystem.FileMode;
            import flash.filesystem.FileStream;
            import flash.filesystem.File;
            import flash.net.registerClassAlias;


            private var data_file:File;

            private function onCreationComplete( ):void
            {
              registerClassAlias("flash.utils.Dictionary",
                                 Dictionary);

              data_file =
                File.appStorageDirectory.resolve("data.db");
            }

            private function
              onSerializeClick(event:MouseEvent):void
            {
                var d:Dictionary = new Dictionary( );
                    d["key_a"] = "value_a";
                    d["key_b"] = "value_b";
                    d["key_c"] = "value_c";
                    d["key_d"] = "value_d";

                var fs:FileStream = new FileStream( );
                    fs.open(data_file, FileMode.WRITE);
                    fs.writeObject(d);
                    fs.close( );

                    outfield.text += "Dictionary Serialized
                      to : " + data_file.nativePath + "\n";
            }

            private function
              onDeserializeClick(event:MouseEvent):void
```

```
{
    var d:Dictionary;

    if(!data_file.exists)
    {
        outfield.text += "Serialized Data File
          does not exist :
          " + data_file.nativePath + "\n";
    }

    var fs:FileStream = new FileStream( );
        fs.open(data_file, FileMode.READ);
        d = (fs.readObject( ) as Dictionary);
        fs.close( );

        outfield.text +=
          "Dictionary de-serialized\n";

        for (var key:String in d)
        {
            outfield.text += key + " :
              " + d[key] + "\n";
        }

}


    ]]>
</mx:Script>
<mx:TextArea id="outfield" left="10" right="10"
  top="10" bottom="62"/>
<mx:Button label="Serialize" bottom="10" right="21"
  click="onSerializeClick(event)"/>
<mx:Button label="Deserialize" bottom="10" right="103"
  click="onDeserializeClick(event)"/>
</mx:ApolloApplication>
```

You can see the serialization in action by:

1. Running the application.
2. Serializing the data by pressing the Serialize button.
3. Restarting the application.
4. Loading and de-serializing the data by pressing the De-serialize button

The data is there even though the application restarted.

Browsing for a File

Problem

You want to use the Apollo Flex components to easily set up code to browse for a file.

Solution

Use one of these Flex components for working with the file system:

```
FileSystemComboBox
FileSystemDataGrid
FileSystemHistoryButton
FileSystemList
FileSystemTree
```

All provide the same user interface on both Mac OS and Windows.

TIP

The Apollo Alpha 1 build has some limited support for using native dialogs to browse for and save files. Full support will be available by the 1.0 release.

Discussion

This example uses the FileSystemTree component, which lets you browse through the files on your computer. Additionally, there is a Button component labeled "Get Info," and a TextArea component for displaying information about the selected item. See Figure 5-1.

The doubleClick event of the FileSystemTree component and the click event of the Button ("Get Info") call the getDetails() method:

```
<mx:FileSystemTree id="tree" height="100%" width="100%"
  doubleClick="getDetails()"/>
<mx:Button label="Get Info" click="getDetails()" />
```

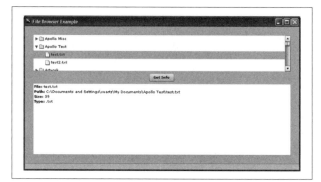

Figure 5-1. File browser example

The getDetails( ) method checks to see if an item is selected in the FileSystemTree component. If so, it calls either the logFileDetails( ) method or the logDirectoryDetails( ) method:

```
public function getDetails():void {
    var node:File = tree.selectedItem as File;
    if(node != null) {
        if(node.isDirectory) {
            logDirectoryDetails(node);
        } else {
            logFileDetails(node);
        }
    }
}
```

The logFileDetails( ) method and the logDirectoryDetails( ) method report details about the selected item in the Text component:

```
public function logFileDetails(file:File):void {
        infoTxt.htmlText = "<b>File:</b> " + file.name + "\n";
        infoTxt.htmlText += "<p><b>Path:</b> " + file.nativePath + "\n";
        infoTxt.htmlText += "<p><b>Size:</b> " + file.size + "\n";
        var fileType:String =
          file.url.substr(file.url.lastIndexOf("."));
        infoTxt.htmlText +=
          "<p><b>Type:</b> " + fileType + "\n";
```

```
        }
        public function logDirectoryDetails(dir:File):void {
                infoTxt.htmlText =
                    "<p><b>Directory:</b> " + dir.name + "\n";
                infoTxt.htmlText += "<p><b>Path:</b> " +
                dir.nativePath ;
        }
```

Note that you may choose to use other Flex file components such as:

```
FileSystemComboBox
FileSystemDataGrid
FileSystemHistoryButton
FileSystemList
```

or a combination of these, depending on your requirements.

Here is the complete MXML code for the example:

```
<?xml version="1.0" encoding="utf-8"?>
<mx:ApolloApplication xmlns:mx="http://www.adobe.com/2006/
mxml" layout="vertical" applicationComplete="init()">
    <mx:Script>
        <![CDATA[
            import flash.filesystem.File;
            public function init():void {
                tree.directory = File.documentsDirectory;
            }
            public function getDetails():void {
                var node:File = tree.selectedItem as File;
                if(node != null) {
                    if(node.isDirectory) {
                        logDirectoryDetails(node);
                    } else {
                        logFileDetails(node);
                    }
                }
            }
            public function logFileDetails(file:File):void {
                    infoTxt.htmlText =
                        "<b>File:</b> " + file.name + "\n";
                    infoTxt.htmlText += "<p><b>Path:</b> "
                    + file.nativePath + "\n";
                    infoTxt.htmlText += "<p><b>Size:</b> "
                    + file.size + "\n";
```

```
                        var fileType:String =
                    file.url.substr(file.url.lastIndexOf("."));
                    infoTxt.htmlText +=
                        "<p><b>Type:</b> " + fileType + "\n";
            }
          public function logDirectoryDetails(dir:File):void {
                    infoTxt.htmlText =
                        "<p><b>Directory:</b> " + dir.name + "\n";
                    infoTxt.htmlText +=
                        "<p><b>Path:</b> " + dir.nativePath ;
            }
        ]]>
    </mx:Script>
    <mx:FileSystemTree id="tree" height="100%"
  width="100%" doubleClick="getDetails()"/>
    <mx:Button label="Get Info" click="getDetails()" />
    <mx:TextArea id="infoTxt" width="100%" height="200"/>
</mx:ApolloApplication>
```

Getting a Directory Listing

Problem

You want to have an ActionScript array listing the contents
of a directory.

Solution

Use the listDirectory( ) method of a File object that points
to a directory. It returns an array of File objects corresponding to files in the directory.

Discussion

You can use the static properties of the File class and the
resolve( ) method to get a File object that points to the
directory you want t

o list. (For more information, see "Accessing Files and Directories" in Chapter 4.) For example, the following code sets a
File object named directory to point to the Apollo Test subdirectory of the user's *documents* directory:

```
var directory:File = File.documentsDirectory.
resolve("Apollo Test");
```

You can then use the listDirectory( ) method to get a list of directory contents:

```
var fileList:Array = directory.listDirectory( );
```

Before calling listDirectory( ), you may want to check whether the directory exists, and that the File object does in fact point to a directory and not a file. You can check the exists and isDirectory properties of the directory object, as in the following code:

```
if (directory.exists && directory.isDirectory) {
    var fileList = directory.listDirectory( );
}
```

You can also use the listDirectoryAsync( ) method if you want other ActionScript code to execute as the directory list is built. The File object (representing the directory) will dispatch a directoryListing event when the directory list is ready. The directoryListing event includes a files property that is an array of File objects corresponding to the files in the directory. The following code shows how to obtain a directory listing asynchronously:

```
var directory:File =
  File.documentsDirectory.resolve("Apollo Test");
if(directory.isDirectory && directory.exists) {
    directory.listDirectoryAsync( );
    directory.addEventListener(FileListEvent.DIRECTORY_LISTING,
                               directoryListHandler);
}
var fileList:Array;

private function directoryListHandler(event:
FileListEvent):void {
    fileList = event.files;
}
```

Figure 5-2 shows a simple application that calculates the size of all files at the root level of a directory selected in the Flex FileSystemTree component.

Figure 5-2. Directory list

Here is the MXML source code for the application:

```xml
<?xml version="1.0" encoding="utf-8"?>
<mx:ApolloApplication
  xmlns:mx= "http://www.adobe.com/2006/mxml"
   layout="vertical"
   applicationComplete="init( )"
   title="Directory List Example">
   <mx:Script>
       <![CDATA[
           import flash.filesystem.File;
           public function init( ):void {
               tree.directory = File.documentsDirectory;
           }
           public function getDetails( ):void {
               var node:File = tree.selectedItem as File;
               if(node != null && node.isDirectory) {
                       calculateRootSize(node);
               }
           }
```

```
            public function calculateRootSize(dir:File):void {
                var size:Number = 0;
                var files:Array = dir.listDirectory(
);
                for (var i:uint; i < files.length; i++) {
                    if (!files[i].isDirectory) {
                        size += files[i].size;
                    }
                }
                infoTxt.htmlText =
                  "<p><b>Directory:</b> " + dir.name
                          + "\n";
                infoTxt.htmlText +=
                  "<p><b>Path:</b> " + dir.nativePath
                          + "\n" ;
                infoTxt.htmlText +=
                  "<p><b>Total Root File Size:</b> "
                          + size + " bytes";
            }
        ]]>
    </mx:Script>
    <mx:FileSystemTree id="tree" height="100%"
      width="100%"/>
    <mx:Button label="Calculate Root File Size"
      click= "getDetails()" />
    <mx:TextArea id="infoTxt" width="100%" height="100"/>
</mx:ApolloApplication>
```

Working with HTML

The Flex HTML control and the HTMLControl class in Action-
Script 3.0 provide advanced HTML capabilities in the Apollo
runtime. This section provides some basic examples. For
more information, see Chapter 3, "Using HTML Within Flex-
Based Apollo Applications."

Recognizing When a Page Has Fully Loaded

Problem

You want to access the content of an HTML page once it has
fully loaded.

Solution

Listen for the complete event that is dispatched by the HTML component after a web page has been fully loaded and rendered, and wait until that event is received before trying to retrieve or alter the HTML content.

Discussion

The following code shows a simple application that shows how to listen for and respond to the complete event:

```
<?xml version="1.0" encoding="utf-8"?>
<mx:ApolloApplication xmlns:mx="http://www.adobe.com/2006/mxml"
    layout="vertical">
    <mx:Script>
    <![CDATA[
        public function onHtmlComplete():void
        {
            var title:String = html.javascriptDocument.title;
            trace("Loaded the page titled: " + title);
        }
    ]]>
    </mx:Script>
    <mx:HTML id="html" width="100%" height="100%"
        location="http://www.oreilly.com"
        complete="onHtmlComplete()" />
</mx:ApolloApplication>
```

When the complete event is received, the onHtmlComplete() method will execute. At this stage, all of the HTML has been loaded and rendered, so the onHtmlComplete() method can obtain and display the loaded page title using the javascriptDocument property.

Altering the Appearance of the HTML Component

Problem

You want to apply interesting visual effects to an HTML page after it has been rendered.

Solution

Use filters or geometric transformations and set some of the appearance-changing properties inherited from the DisplayObject class.

Discussion

Because the Flex HTML component is a display object, you can use any of the properties and methods of the ActionScript DisplayObject class with an HTML component (or with the underlying HTMLControl object). These include the filters and rotation and alpha properties, just to name a few.

For example, you can apply a ColorMatrixFilter filter to an HTML control, and use Flex HSlider controls to adjust the red, green, blue, and alpha levels that the filter controls, as seen in Figure 5-3.

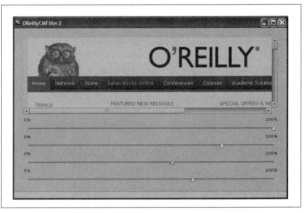

Figure 5-3. HSlider in action

When the value of any of the sliders change, the changeFilter() method is called and applies a ColorMatrixFilter filter based on the values of the sliders:

```
public function setCMFilter():void {
    var matrix:Array = new Array();
```

```
    matrix = matrix.concat([redSlider.value, 0, 0, 0, 0]); // red
    matrix = matrix.concat([0, greenSlider.value, 0, 0, 0]); // green
    matrix = matrix.concat([0, 0, blueSlider.value, 0, 0]); // blue
    matrix = matrix.concat([0, 0, 0, alphaSlider.value, 0]); // alpha
    var cmFilter:ColorMatrixFilter = new ColorMatrixFilter(matrix);
    html.filters = [cmFilter];
}
```

The following example shows the complete MXML and
ActionScript source code for the application:

```
<?xml version="1.0" encoding="utf-8"?>
<mx:ApolloApplication
xmlns:mx="http://www.adobe.com/2006/mxml"
layout="vertical" alpha="1">
    <mx:Script>
    <![CDATA[
      public function setCMFilter():void {
        var matrix:Array = new Array();
        matrix = matrix.concat([redSlider.value, 0, 0, 0, 0]); // r
        matrix = matrix.concat([0, greenSlider.value, 0, 0, 0]); // g
        matrix = matrix.concat([0, 0, blueSlider.value, 0, 0]); // b
        matrix = matrix.concat([0, 0, 0, alphaSlider.value, 0]); // a
        var cmFilter:ColorMatrixFilter =
          new ColorMatrixFilter(matrix);
        html.filters = [cmFilter];
        }
    ]]>
    </mx:Script>
    <mx:HTML id="html" location="http://www.oreilly.com"
        width="100%" height="100%" />
    <mx:HSlider value="1" width="100%" id="redSlider"
      minimum="0" maximum="1" labels="['0%', '100%']" change="setCMFilter()" />
    <mx:HSlider value="1" width="100%" id="greenSlider"
        minimum="0" maximum="1" labels=
          "['0%', '100%']" change="setCMFilter()" />
    <mx:HSlider value="1" width="100%" id="blueSlider"
        minimum="0" maximum="1" labels=
          "['0%', '100%']" change="setCMFilter()" />
    <mx:HSlider value="1" width="100%" id="alphaSlider"
        minimum="0" maximum="1" labels="['0%', '100%']"
change="setCMFilter()" />
</mx:ApolloApplication>
```

Using the Windowing API

The Apollo Window API lets you create applications that use custom chrome and background transparency.

You can also use system chrome (Figure 5-4), the standard window design used by Mac OS and Windows.

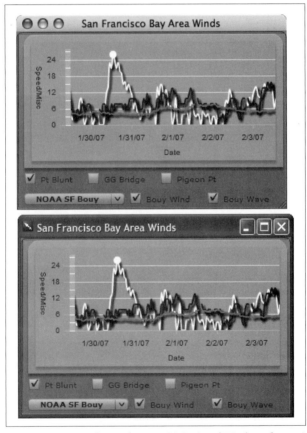

Figure 5-4. System chrome for Mac OS (top) and Windows (bottom)

You can also define your own chrome (Figure 5-5), which may use a semi-transparent background for the application.

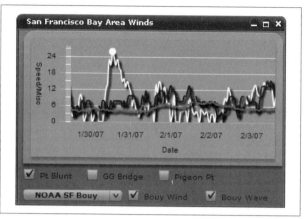

Figure 5-5. Custom chrome

TIP

Multiple Native Window support was slated to be included in the Apollo Alpha 1 build. However, this may have changed between the time the book was written and the build was published. Check the Apollo documentation for the most recent information.

The next section gives examples that show how to work with the Windowing API.

Making a Window Transparent

Problem

You want your application to have a semi-transparent background.

Solution

Set the systemChrome setting to "none" and the transparent setting to "true" in the application descriptor file, and set the alpha of the root component of the application to a number between 0 and 1.

Discussion

The application descriptor file (also known as the *application.xml* file) includes a setting for setting the chrome and transparency of the main window of an application:

systemChrome
> You can set this to "standard" to have the application use the standard window chrome for the system, or to "none" to define your own window chrome.

transparent
> If you set the systemChrome setting to "none", you can set transparent to "true" which lets you apply a semi-transparent background for the application window. (You will want to apply a setting for the alpha property of the root component in the MXML code.)

The application descriptor file defines settings for the application.

Set the systemChrome and transparent attribute of the rootContent property of the *application.xml* file (the application descriptor file) for the application, as in the following:

```
<?xml version="1.0" encoding="UTF-8"?>
<application
  xmlns="http://ns.adobe.com/apollo/application/1.0.M3"
  appId="com.oreilly.apollo.examples.SampleTransparent"
  version="1.0">
  <properties>
    <name>Sample Transparent Application</name>
    <publisher>Acme Apollo Apps, Inc</publisher>
    <description>A sample application</description>
    <copyright>(c)2007</copyright>
  </properties>
```

```
<rootContent systemChrome="none" transparent="true"
    visible="true">main.swf</rootContent>
</application>
```

Then, in the root ApolloApplication tag for your application, set the alpha property to "0.5" (for 50% transparency)
or any number between 0 and 1:

```
<?xml version="1.0" encoding="utf-8"?>
<mx:ApolloApplication
    xmlns:mx="http://www.adobe.com/2006/mxml"
    layout="vertical"
    title="Transparency Test"
    alpha="0.5">
    <mx:TextArea
        text="Note the tranparency."
        textAlign="center"
        width="100%"
        height="100%"/>
</mx:ApolloApplication>
```

Using Your Own Window Chrome Elements

Problem

You want to jazz up your application's user interface with
customized buttons that minimize, maximize, restore, and
close the application window.

Solution

Set the systemChrome attribute to "none" and the transparent
attribute to "true" in the application descriptor file. Then
create your own buttons or other user interface components
that call the minimize( ), maximize( ), restore( ), and close( )
methods of the window object.

Discussion

By default, the systemChrome attribute of a new Apollo application is set to "standard". This tells the application to display the standard set of window chrome elements, such as
the title bar and buttons to minimize, maximize, and close

the window, for the operating system on which the application is running.

If you want to display your own set of window chrome elements, you should first change the `systemChrome` attribute to `"none"` in the application descriptor file. Additionally, if you want the application to have a semi-transparent background, set the `transparent` attribute to `"true"` and apply an `alpha` setting between 0 and 1 in the root component of the MXML code. For details on how to change this setting, see the earlier section "Making a Window Transparent."

As you lay out the user interface for your application, make sure that the containers and interface elements will stretch to fit the application window when it changes size.

Next you'll need to create the interface elements that trigger the minimizing, maximizing, and closing of the window. In most cases, these elements will be buttons—as in the following example, which uses three instances of the Flex Button control.

To minimize the window, the application should call the `NativeWindow.minimize()` method. The operating system usually handles the task of restoring the window to its previous size when the user clicks on a small button or icon that represents the minimized application. However, if you want the window to be restored in response to another event, such as receiving a request from a remote server, the application can call the `NativeWindow.restore()` method directly.

To maximize the window, the application can call the `NativeWindow.maximize()` method. `NativeWindow.restore()` can also be used to return a maximized window to its previous size and position.

Finally, calling the `NativeWindow.close()` method starts the process of closing the window and stopping the application.

The following example displays three buttons in the upper-right corner of the window, for minimizing, maximizing, and closing the application window. The buttons themselves are very simple, using text characters in place of icons. A more attractive set of buttons would use nice graphics as icons. The example also uses some CSS style declarations to give the interface elements a simple desktop application look and feel:

```xml
<?xml version="1.0" encoding="utf-8"?>
<mx:Application xmlns:mx="http://www.adobe.com/2006/mxml"
    creationComplete="initApp()"
    layout="vertical" verticalGap="0">

    <mx:Style>
        Application {
            backgroundColor:#669977;
            paddingLeft: 2;
            paddingRight: 2;
            paddingTop: 3;
            paddingBottom: 2;
            borderStyle: outset;
        }
        .windowTitleBar {
            backgroundColor: #006633;
            fontFamily: Georgia,"Times New Roman",Times,serif;
            fontSize: 12;
            fontWeight: bold;
            color: #FFFFFF;
            paddingLeft: 3;
            paddingRight: 3;
            paddingTop: 3;
        }
        .chromeBtn {
            fontFamily: Verdana,Arial,Helvetica,sans;
            fontSize: 10;
        }
        .contentBox {
            backgroundColor: #FFFFFF;
            backgroundAlpha:0.7;
        }
    </mx:Style>

    <mx:Script>
    <![CDATA[
        public var isMaximized:Boolean = false;
```

```
private function onMinimizeBtn(evt:MouseEvent):void
{
    stage.window.minimize();
}

private function onMaximizeBtn(evt:MouseEvent):void
{
    if (this.isMaximized)
    {
        stage.window.restore();
        this.isMaximized = false;
    }
    else
    {
        stage.window.maximize();
        this.isMaximized = true;
    }
}

private function onCloseBtn(evt:MouseEvent):void
{
    stage.window.close();
}

]]>
</mx:Script>

<mx:HBox id="windowTitleBar" width="100%"
    horizontalGap="1" styleName="windowTitleBar">

    <mx:Label id="windowTitleTxt" width="100%"
        text="Custom Window Chrome Example" />

    <mx:Button id="minimizeBtn" label="_"
        width="20" height="16"
        styleName="chromeBtn"
        click="onMinimizeBtn(event)" />

        <mx:Button id="maximizeBtn" label='{"\u25A2"}'
            width="20" height="16"
            styleName="chromeBtn"
            click="onMaximizeBtn(event)" />
```

```
                    <mx:Button id="closeBtn" label="X"
                        width="20" height="16"
                        styleName="chromeBtn"
                        click="onCloseBtn(event)" />
                </mx:HBox>

                <mx:VBox id="contentBox" styleName="contentBox"
                    width="100%" height="100%" />

    </mx:Application>
```

Moving and Resizing a Window That Uses Custom Chrome

Problem

Your window is not using system chrome elements, but you want the window to be movable and resizable.

Solution

Listen for mouseDown events at specific locations in the window and call the NativeWindow.startMove( ) method or the Window.resize( ) method, as appropriate.

Discussion

When the systemChrome attribute is set to "none" in the application descriptor file, the resulting window will not have built-in support for moving and resizing.

In most cases, the window moving process and the window resizing process should begin when the user presses the mouse button. Your application can listen for the mouseDown event to know when the mouse button is pressed, and then check the location of the cursor to see if the user intends to move or resize the window.

In the following example code, a click in the title bar of the window starts the move process, while a click near the outer borders of the window starts the resize process.

The example limits the area used for triggering a move by listening only for `mouseDown` events in the `windowTitleBar` container, like this:

```
this.windowTitleBar.addEventListener(MouseEvent.MOUSE_DOWN,
                          onMouseDownInTitleBar);
```

The `onMouseDownInTitleBar( )` method calls the `NativeWindow.startMove( )` method to begin the process of moving the window in concert with the mouse cursor, for as long as the user keeps the mouse button pressed. When the mouse button is released, the window stops moving.

Your application needs only to initiate the window moving process. The runtime handles the actual movement of the window and stops it when the mouse button is released.

For trigger resizing, the application listens for a `mouseDown` event anywhere in its main window, like this:

```
this.addEventListener(MouseEvent.MOUSE_DOWN,
onMouseDownInWindow);
```

The `onMouseDownInWindow( )` method then tests to see if the location of the cursor is below the title bar and within 20 pixels of the outer edge of the window. If so, it determines which directions the resizing can take and calls the `NativeWindow.resize( )` method accordingly.

As with moving, your application needs only to initiate the resizing process. The runtime takes care of stretching the window boundaries and stopping them when the mouse button is released.

Here is the full source code for the example. This example retains the styling and the close button from the example shown earlier in the section "Using Your Own Window Chrome Elements":

```
<?xml version="1.0" encoding="utf-8"?>
<mx:Application xmlns:mx="http://www.adobe.com/2006/mxml"
  creationComplete="initApp( )"
```

```
    layout="vertical"
    verticalGap="0">

<mx:Style>
  Application {
    backgroundColor:#669977;
    paddingLeft: 2;
    paddingRight: 2;
    paddingTop: 3;
    paddingBottom: 2;
    borderStyle: outset;
  }
  .windowTitleBar {
    backgroundColor: #006633;
    fontFamily: Georgia, "Times New Roman", Times, serif;
    fontSize: 12;
    fontWeight: bold;
    color: #FFFFFF;
    paddingLeft: 3;
    paddingRight: 3;
    paddingTop: 3;
  }
  .chromeBtn {
    fontFamily: Verdana, Arial, Helvetica, sans;
    fontSize: 10;
  }
  .contentBox {
    backgroundColor: #FFFFFF;
    backgroundAlpha:0.7;
  }
</mx:Style>

<mx:Script>
<![CDATA[
  import mx.events.ResizeEvent;

  public var isMaximized:Boolean = false;
  public static var RESIZE_HANDLE_WIDTH:int = 20;

  private function initApp( ):void {
    // The user can move the window by holding the mouse
    // down over the title bar only
    this.windowTitleBar.addEventListener(MouseEvent.MOUSE_DOWN,
                                   onMouseDownInTitleBar);
```

```
      // The user can resize by clicking and dragging in the
      // outer margins of the window below the title bar
      this.addEventListener(MouseEvent.MOUSE_DOWN,
                            onMouseDownInWindow);
}

private function
  onMouseDownInTitleBar(evt:MouseEvent):void {
  stage.window.startMove();
}

private function onMouseDownInWindow(evt:MouseEvent):void {
  var xPos:Number = evt.stageX;
  var yPos:Number = evt.stageY;
  var resizeDirection:String = NativeWindowResize.NONE;

  if (!this.isMaximized && yPos > this.windowTitleBar.height) {
    if (yPos > this.height - RESIZE_HANDLE_WIDTH) {
      // It will resize to the bottom
      if (xPos > this.width - RESIZE_HANDLE_WIDTH) {
        // It will also resize to the right
        resizeDirection =
          NativeWindowResize.BOTTOM_RIGHT;
      }
      else if (xPos < RESIZE_HANDLE_WIDTH) {
        // It will also resize to the left
        resizeDirection = NativeWindowResize.BOTTOM_LEFT;
      }
      else {
        resizeDirection = WindowResize.BOTTOM;
      }
    }
    else {
      // No vertical resizing
      if (xPos > this.width - RESIZE_HANDLE_WIDTH) {
        // Only resize to the right
        resizeDirection = NativeWindowResize.RIGHT;
      }
      else if (xPos < RESIZE_HANDLE_WIDTH) {
        // Only resize to the left
        resizeDirection = NativeWindowResize.LEFT;
      }
    }

    if (resizeDirection != NativeWindowResize.NONE) {
      stage.window.startResize(resizeDirection);
```

```
        }
      }
    }

    private function onCloseBtn(evt:MouseEvent):void {
      stage.window.close();
    }
  ]]>
</mx:Script>

<mx:HBox id="windowTitleBar" width="100%"
  horizontalGap="1" styleName="windowTitleBar">

  <mx:Label id="windowTitleTxt" width="100%"
    text="Moving and Resizing Example" />

  <mx:Button id="closeBtn" label="X"
    width="20" height="16"
    styleName="chromeBtn"
    click="onCloseBtn(event)" />
</mx:HBox>

<mx:VBox id="contentBox" styleName="contentBox"
  width="100%" height="100%" />

</mx:Application>
```

An obvious enhancement is to make the change the shape of the mouse cursor when it is over an area that can trigger resizing, but that will be left to the reader.

Making a Window Cast a Shadow on the Desktop

Problem

You want the border of the main window of the application to cast a drop shadow on the desktop and background applications.

Solution

Set the systemChrome setting to "none" and the transparent setting to "true" in the application descriptor file, and set the dropShadowEnabled and dropShadowColor styles of the ApolloApplication component.

Discussion

An Apollo application that is set to use custom chrome can cast a shadow on the borders of the main window, as shown in Figure 5-6.

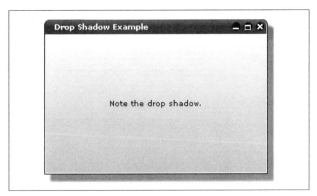

Figure 5-6. Drop shadow

First, be sure to set the systemChrome setting to "none" and the transparent setting to "true" in the application settings. In Flex Builder, do this in the final step of the New Apollo Project dialog box. If you are using the Apollo SDK, set this in the systemChrome and transparent attributes of the rootContent property of the application descriptor file (*application.xml*), as in the following:

```
<application
  xmlns="http://ns.adobe.com/apollo/application/1.0.M3"
  appId="com.oreilly.apollo.examples.DropShadow"
  version="1.0">
  <properties>
    <name>OReillyDropShadow</name>
    <publisher>Acme Apollo Apps, Inc.</publisher>
  </properties>
  <rootContent systemChrome="none" transparent="true"
    visible="true">
    DropShadowTest.swf
  </rootContent>
</application>
```

For more information, see the earlier section "Making a Window Transparent."

Next, in the root ApolloApplication tag in the MXML code, declare values for the dropShadowEnabled, dropShadowColor, shadowDirection, and shadowDistance styles:

```
dropShadowColor="0xFF00FF" dropShadowEnabled="true"
shadowDirection="right" shadowDistance="10"
```

These define the settings for the shadow.

Here is the complete MXML code for the example:

```
<?xml version="1.0" encoding="utf-8"?>
<mx:ApolloApplication
xmlns:mx="http://www.adobe.com/2006/mxml" layout="absolute"
    dropShadowColor="0xFF00FF" dropShadowEnabled="true"
    shadowDirection="right" shadowDistance="10"
    backgroundColor="0xFFFFFF"
    height="200" width="300" title="Drop Shadow Example">

    <mx:Text text="Note the drop shadow."
verticalCenter="0" horizontalCenter="0"/>

</mx:ApolloApplication>
```

Saving and Restoring the Size and Position of a Window

Problem

You want to save the position and size of a window to a preferences file, and then use the last saved values to define the position and size when the application starts up again.

Solution

Save the bounds property of the NativeWindow object to a file and read the property from the file upon startup.

Discussion

The Apollo Window API includes methods for resizing and repositioning windows.

This example stores the coordinates of the window to a preferences file every time the user repositions or resizes the window.

The NativeWindow object for any display object can be obtained by the window property of the stage property of the display object:

```
stage.window
```

When the user resizes or repositions the window, the window dispatches a move or resize event. The init( ) method of our sample (executed when the application is rendered), sets up event listeners for these events:

```
stage.window.addEventListener(NativeWindowBoundsEvent.MOVE,
                    setMouseUpHandler);
stage.window.addEventListener(NativeWindowBoundsEvent.RESIZE,
                    setMouseUpHandler);
```

The setMouseUpHandler( ) method listens for the mouseUp event:

```
public function setMouseUpHandler(event:
NativeWindowBoundsEvent):void {
    this.addEventListener(MouseEvent.MOUSE_UP, saveData);
}
```

The NativeWindow object has a bounds property that defines the coordinates and size of the window:

```
stage.window.bounds
```

The bounds property is a Rectangle object defining the window boundaries. The Rectangle class is defined in the flash.geom package.

When the user releases the mouse (and the window is resized or repositioned), the saveData( ) method writes the bounds property of the NativeWindow object to a file, defined by the prefs File object:

```
private function saveData(event:MouseEvent):void {
    stage.window.removeEventListener(MouseEvent.MOUSE_UP, saveData);
    var stream:FileStream = new FileStream( );
```

```
        stream.open(prefs, FileMode.WRITE);
        stream.writeObject(stage.window.bounds);
        stream.close( );
    }
```

The init( ) method of our sample also checks to see if the preferences file exists. If it does, the application has previously stored the bounds property of the NativeWindow object to that file. It then reads that file and adjusts the bounds property of the NativeWindow object to match the values set in the file:

```
if (prefs.exists) {
    var stream:FileStream = new FileStream( );
    stream.open(prefs, FileMode.READ);
    var bounds:Rectangle = stream.readObject( );
    stage.window.bounds = bounds;
    stream.close( );
}
```

For information on how the File and FileStream objects operate in this application in order to read and write an object to a file, see the earlier section "Serializing and De-Serializing ActionScript Objects to the File System."

Here is the complete MXML code for this sample application:

```
<?xml version="1.0" encoding="utf-8"?>
<mx:ApolloApplication xmlns:mx="http://www.adobe.com/2006/
mxml" layout="vertical" applicationComplete="init( )">
    <mx:Script>
        <![CDATA[
            import flash.net.registerClassAlias;
            import flash.filesystem.*;
            public var prefs:File =
              File.appStorageDirectory.resolve("windowState.amf");

            public function init( ):void {
              flash.net.registerClassAlias("flash.geom.Rectangle",
              Rectangle);
              flash.net.registerClassAlias("flash.geom.Point",
              Point);
                if (prefs.exists) {
                  var stream:FileStream = new FileStream( );
                    stream.open(prefs, FileMode.READ);
```

```
                    var bounds:Rectangle = stream.readObject();
                       stage.window.bounds = bounds;
                       stream.close();
                  }
                 stage.window.
                   addEventListener(NativeWindowBoundsEvent.MOVE,
                                             setMouseUpHandler);
                stage.window.
                   addEventListener(NativeWindowBoundsEvent.RESIZE,
                                             setMouseUpHandler);
              }
             public function
               setMouseUpHandler(event:WindowBoundsEvent):void {
                 this.addEventListener(MouseEvent.MOUSE_UP,
                 saveData);
               }
            private function saveData(event:MouseEvent):void {
                 stage.window.
removeEventListener(MouseEvent.MOUSE_UP, saveData);
                 var stream:FileStream = new FileStream();
                 stream.open(prefs, FileMode.WRITE);
                 stream.writeObject(stage.window.bounds);
                 stream.close();
             }
          ]]>
      </mx:Script>
      <mx:TextArea width="100%" height="100%"
textAlign="center" >
         <mx:text>Drag the window corners to resize and
reposition it.</mx:text>
      </mx:TextArea>
</mx:ApolloApplication>
```

Apollo Packages and Classes

Table A-1 lists the new ActionScript packages and classes that are part of the Apollo Alpha 1 release.

Table A-1. Apollo ActionScript classes

Package	Classes
flash.display	flash.display.NativeWindow
	flash.display.NativeWindowDisplayState
	flash.display.NativeWindowIcon
	flash.display.NativeWindowInitOptions
	flash.display.NativeWindowResize
	flash.display.NativeWindowSystemChrome
flash.events	flash.events.FileListEvent
	flash.events.InvokeEvent
	flash.eventsHTMLUncaughtJavaScriptExceptionEvent
	flash.events.NativeWindowBoundsEvent
	flash.events.NativeWindowDisplayStateEvent
	flash.events.NativeWindowErrorEvent
flash.filesystem	flash.filesystem.File
	flash.filesystem.FileMode
	flash.filesystem.FileStream
flash.html	flash.html.HTMLControl
	flash.html.JavaScriptFunction
	flash.html.script.JavaScriptObject
flash.system	flash.system.Shell
	flash.system.NativeWindowCapabilities
	flash.system.Updater

Table A-2 lists the Flex Apollo component classes.

Table A-2. Flex Apollo component classes

Package	Classes
mx.core	mx.core.ApolloApplication
mx.controls	mx.controls.FileSystemComboBox mx.controls.FileSystemDataGrid mx.controls.FileSystemEnumerationMode mx.controls.FileSystemHistoryButton mx.controls.FileSystemList mx.controls.FileSystemSizeDisplayMode mx.controls.FileSystemTree mx.controls.HTML

A few core ActionScript classes have been altered to support Apollo. Table A-3 lists the classes that have changed and the new methods or properties that they offer.

Table A-3. Changes to existing classes for Apollo

Class	New Property or Method
flash.display.Stage	window property
flash.events.Event	DOM_INITIALIZE constant HTML_BOUNDS_CHANGE constant HTML_RENDER constant LOCATION_CHANGE constant NETWORK_CHANGE constant
flash.system.Security	APPLICATION constant
flash.utils.ByteArray	deflate() method inflate() method
flash.net.URLRequest	followRedirects manageCookies shouldAuthenticate shouldCacheResponse useCache

Apollo Command-Line Tools

The Apollo SDK provides the following command-line tools:

AMXMLC
> A command-line wrapper for the MXMLC compiler that configures the compiler to use Apollo classes.

ADL
> Use this tool to launch and test an Apollo application without having to install it.

ADT
> Use this tool to package an Apollo application into a redistributable AIR file.

These tools are also available in the Apollo Extensions for Flex Builder. They are installed in the *bin* subdirectory.

This Appendix lists the options for each of the command-line tools.

For an example of using these tools, see Chapter 2.

AMXMLC

AMXMLC is a simple wrapper for the MXMLC Flex compiler, which links in the appropriate Apollo-specific libraries.

Usage is the same as MXMLC:

```
amxmlc myTestApp.mxml
```

This shell script is included in the *bin* directory of the Apollo SDK directory.

The first argument passed to the compiler is the location of the MXML file to compile (*myTestApp.mxml* in the previous example).

There are a number of other options for the MXMLC compiler. For details on these, see:

   http://livedocs.macromedia.com/flex/201/html/compilers_123_24.html

ADL

ADL is a command-line tool that launches an Apollo application, based on it's *application.xml* file, without requiring that the application be installed. This is useful for testing and debugging the application.

Typically, you want to call the ADL tool passing one parameter: the path to the application descriptor file (the application.*xml* file):

```
adl application.xml
```

The full syntax of the ADL command is:

```
adl ( -runtime <path-to-runtime-dir> )? <path-to-app-xml>
<path-to-root-dir>? ( -- ... )?
```

Here is a description of the command-line arguments for ADL:

Option	Description
-runtime	Optional argument that specifies the directory that contains the Apollo runtime that should be used.
path-app-xml	The *application.xml* descriptor file for the application that should be launched.
path-to-root-dir	Optional argument that specifies the directory that contains the *application.xml* descriptor file
--	Any arguments specified after this argument will be passed to the application as startup/command-line arguments.

ADT

ADT is a command-line tool that packages Apollo applications into redistributable AIR files. The Apollo runtime can then install the Apollo application from that AIR file.

Typically, you want to call the ADT tool in the following way:

```
adt –package HelloWorld.air application.xml HelloWorld.swf
```

In this example, the ADT tool creates an AIR file named *HelloWorld.air* based on the *application.xml* application descriptor file.

The syntax of the ADT command is the following:

```
adt -package <air-file> <app-xml> <fileOrDir>* ( -C <dir>
<fileOrDir>+ )*
```

Here are the command-line options for ADT:

Option	Description
-package	The first argument must be -package.
air-file	The relative or absolute path to the AIR to be created by ADT.
app-xml	The relative or absolute path to the *appliction.xml* descriptor file for the application.
fileOrDir	One or more file or directory names identifying other files to be included in the package. Each successive file or directory name should be separated by a space.
	If a directory name is specified, then all of the files in that directory and its subdirectories will be included. However, files that are marked hidden in the file system will be ignored.
	If any of the files listed is the same as the file specified in the <app.xml> parameter, then it will be ignored; it will not be added to the package file a second time.
	These files and directories will be copied into the application install directory when the application is installed.
-C <dir>	This changes the root directory path for subsequent files or directories listed in the command line.

Index

We'd like to hear your suggestions for improving our indexes. Send email to
index@oreilly.com.

Better than e-books

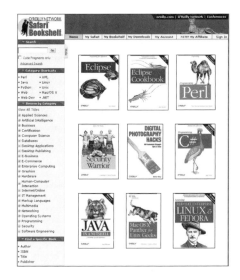

Related Titles from O'Reilly

Web Programming

ActionScript 3 Cookbook

ActionScript for Flash MX: The Definitive Guide, *2nd Edition*

Ajax Design Patterns

Ajax Hacks

Building Scalable Web Sites

Dynamic HTML: The Definitive Reference, *2nd Edition*

Flash Hacks

Essential PHP Security

Google Advertising Tools

Google Hacks, *2nd Edition*

Google Map Hacks

Google Pocket Guide

Google: The Missing Manual, *2nd Edition*

Head First HTML with CSS & XHTML

Head Rush Ajax

HTTP: The Definitive Guide

JavaScript & DHTML Cookbook

JavaScript Pocket Reference, *2nd Edition*

JavaScript: The Definitive Guide, *4th Edition*

Learning PHP 5

Learning PHP and MySQL

PHP Cookbook

PHP Hacks

PHP in a Nutshell

PHP Pocket Reference, *2nd Edition*

PHPUnit Pocket Guide

Programming ColdFusion MX, *2nd Edition*

Programming PHP, *2nd Edition*

Upgrading to PHP 5

Web Database Applications with PHP and MySQL, *2nd Edition*

Web Site Cookbook

Webmaster in a Nutshell, *3rd Edition*

Web Administration

Apache Cookbook

Apache Pocket Reference

Apache: The Definitive Guide, *3rd Edition*

Perl for Web Site Management

Squid: The Definitive Guide

Web Performance Tuning, *2nd Edition*

O'REILLY®

Our books are available at most retail and online bookstores.

To order direct: 1-800-998-9938 • *order@oreilly.com* • *www.oreilly.com*

Online editions of most O'Reilly titles are available by subscription at *safari.oreilly.com*

Related Titles from O'Reilly

Web Authoring and Design

ActionScript 3 Cookbook

Ajax Hacks

Ambient Findability

Cascading Style Sheets: The Definitive Guide, *2nd Edition*

Creating Web Sites: The Missing Manual

CSS Cookbook

CSS Pocket Reference, *2nd Edition*

CSS: The Missing Manual

Dreamweaver 8: Design and Construction

Dreamweaver 8: The Missing Manual

Essential ActionScript 2.0

Flash 8: Projects for Learning Animation and Interactivity

Flash 8: The Missing Manual

Flash Hacks

Head First HTML with CSS & XHTML

Head Rush Ajax

HTML & XHTML: The Definitive Guide, *5th Edition*

HTML & XHTML Pocket Reference, *3rd Edition*

Information Architecture for the World Wide Web, *2nd Edition*

Information Dashboard Design

Learning Web Design, *2nd Edition*

PHP Hacks

Programming Flash Communication Server

Web Design in a Nutshell, *3rd Edition*

Web Site Measurement Hacks

O'REILLY®